EXPRESSIONISM AND FILM

EXPRESSIONISM AND FILM

Rudolf Kurtz

Edited with an afterword by
Christian Kiening and Ulrich Johannes Beil
Translated by Brenda Benthien

British Library Cataloguing in Publication Data

EXPRESSIONISM AND FILM

A catalogue entry for this book is available from the British Library

ISBN: 9780 86196 718 6 (Paperback edition)

Cover illustration: Paul Leni.

Original title: Rudolf Kurtz: *Expressionismus und Film.*
Nachdruck der Ausgabe von 1926. Herausgegeben und mit einem
Nachwort versehen von Christian Kiening und Ulrich Johannes Beil.
Zürich: Chronos 2007, second edition 2011
(Medienwandel – Medienwechsel – Medienwissen, vol. 2).

Published by
John Libbey Publishing Ltd, 3 Leicester Road, New Barnet, Herts EN5 5EW,
United Kingdom
e-mail: john.libbey@orange.fr; web site: www.johnlibbey.com

Distributed worldwide by **Indiana University Press**,
Herman B Wells Library – 350, 1320 E. 10th St., Bloomington, IN 47405, USA.
www.iupress.indiana.edu

Printed and bound in China by 1010 Printing International Ltd.

Foreword

This small book makes a text accessible to the English speaking reader that is not only a classic of film history, but also an important work from the early phase of modern media history. *Expressionismus und Film* by Rudolf Kurtz, which appeared first in 1926 in the *Verlag der Lichtbildbühne* in Berlin (with 73 reproductions, 5 colour plates and a cover illustration by Paul Leni) is a book by a well-known contemporary of the expressionist movement. Written with analytical brilliance and historical vision, it captures Expressionism at the time of its impending conclusion – as an intersection of world view, resoluteness of form, and medial transition. Though there exist translations into French and Italian (without the original illustrations), a long-desired translation into English has not been previously undertaken. The editors are grateful to film expert Brenda Benthien who enthusiastically translated the 1926 original as well as the afterword to the German reprint (2007) which appears here in a revised, slightly shortened and actualized form. They would also like to thank the National Centre of Competence in Research *Mediality – Historical Perspectives* (Zurich) for its financial support, the publisher of the German reprint (Zurich: Chronos) for providing the reproductions of the plates of the 1926 original, and John Libbey, who made it possible to give this book a new home. We are convinced that it has not lost its relevance after ninety years.

Zurich, Summer 2015   Christian Kiening and Ulrich Johannes Beil

Colour Plate I. Walter Reimann, design for *Caligari* (Ufa-Decla Film).

CONTENTS

NB: In the original edition, the table of contents is placed after the dedication to Jannings and the foreword by Kurtz. Kurtz's occasional misspellings of names have been tacitly corrected throughout the text.

TO EMIL JANNINGS

The Man

The Artist

The Friend

The aphoristic nature of this work can be explained by my desire to allow its methodic disposition to prove useful to readers with as wide a range of experience as possible, without overloading the work textually. I am indebted to Walter Harburger, who wrote the chapter on music, as well as Hans Richter and Heinrich Fraenkel, for their friendly assistance. And last, but not least, to my publisher, who provided the stimulus for the work, and made possible its rich illustration.

THE MEANING OF EXPRESSIONISM

Catchwords are coined without their exactly meaning anything. People form them like technical acronyms, making them up out of the first letters of words. *Wumba* [*Waffen- und Munitionsbeschaffungsamt*] and *Priteg* [*Privat-Telefon-Gesellschaft*] are merely suggestive sounds with no content, which can easily be remembered.

If the catchword catches on though, a strange process begins. It takes on colour, meaning, content from the activities to which it refers. The more things it stands for, the more strongly it grasps the public imagination; the longer it remains in use, the more clearly certain characteristics can be extracted from it. If the catchword should manage to make emotional associations come alive, then its meaning becomes more comprehensible through use. Words such as "Classicism", "Romanticism", or "Biedermeier" are by now well-characterized historical descriptors.

The same is true of the much-debated word "Expressionism". When first used at the young painters' conventicles, it was a rallying cry against the prevailing "Impressionism" – a term which itself was coined in much the same way. At first there was no particular programme associated with the word: it arose from a feeling rather than definable thought. But the movement arose at a favourable point in history, and the label stuck. People who use the word "Expressionism" today are convinced that they have conveyed a certain intellectual point of view.

There is no clear definition to be found in the significant body of literature on Expressionism. Psychologists, aestheticians and historians of the phrase dwell more on atmospheric descriptions than on rational definitions. Perhaps the difficulty lies in the fact that Expressionism covers a wealth of phenomena, which only appear uniform by virtue of their confrontation with the Impressionistic point of view which they commonly oppose.

WORLD VIEW

The term "Expressionism" arose in connection with works of fine art. However, our scope would be too narrow if we looked for its defining properties exclusively in the works of painters. If we intend to concern ourselves with something larger than just the playful experiments of a clique, we must recognize the face of this movement in a certain type of modern man.

Expressionism never aspired to be less than a kind of "world view". Works of art do not take shape at the discretion of individuals; they are formed of historic necessity. If Expressionism is to be considered a historic movement, it must bear the hallmark of a particular generation – though its character has also weakened, in accordance with the lives and professions of its representatives.

The problem becomes most apparent when we consider the origin of the word. Expressionism did not protest against painterly details; it demanded a revision of the entirety of human behaviour. Impressionistic man attempted to develop a maximum amount of sensitivity, to capture the momentary impulse, the joy and fate of the instant. It was a matter of sensitive skin, of nuance, of "sensibility". The fleetingness of the impulse stood in inverse relation to the magnitude of the response.

It is the task of historiography to redefine the characteristics of this generation, based on the intellectual activity of the human race to around 1910. Impressionists are sensitive, introspective natures, their emotional lives finding expression in the masterful painting of Manet, their con-

Figure 1. Pablo Picasso, *Nude*; © 2007 ProLitteris, Zurich.

sciences shaped by the characters in the dramatic world of Ibsen. Out of the shadows that cast their reflections on the soul, Strindberg's ghostly diorama takes shape, hovering between world angst and mortal fury. [Karl Gottfried] Lamprecht, in his *Deutsche Geschichte* [*German History*], attempted to explain the behaviour of this type as resulting from

"Reizsamkeit" ["sensibility"], which is just a Germanization of the word "Impressionism". Richard Hamann, in his work on Impressionism [1907] – which wanders through the depth and width of various branches of culture – undertakes to flesh out this type with richer details. Generally speaking, impressionist man is characterized by his belief in the omnipotence of psychology. Empathy and understanding are the bulwarks of his world of understanding, and even metaphysics becomes a function of psychological deliberation.

The antithesis to this focus may be found in Expressionism. The new painters want to get away from the time-bound, away from the moment, away from "impression" and toward creation. It goes without saying that it's unfair nowadays to simply write off impressionist art as lacking creative purpose. But fairness requires the consideration of the morals of history, rather than of active history as it's happening, in catastrophes and explosions.

Expressionism seeks not to passively accept; it seeks to create. This new direction heralds an attitude of the will. The expressionist philosophy unleashes forms of reality – though not by taking them from somehow "photographable" everyday life. The accentuation of the creative is the new embodiment of the European soul. A new type is emerging in art, taking the place of the reflection and the paradoxy of impressionist man. We see it in the machine world of Johannes V. Jensen, the new sports-and-fresh-air people, the paintings by Picasso, and the poetry by Johannes R. Becher. Empathetic, imitative psychology is no longer the handmaiden of art: instead, its creation is determined by metaphysical Will. This attitude is taking hold of all the conventions and spheres of society: through "Organization", the constructive spirit creates the means for the intellectual arrangement of the necessary elements. The emotional element of the work process is forced out, taken apart, and recreated in clear steps, "business management" style. The great economic systems behave similarly, merging horizontally and vertically into cartels, syndicates, and trusts, into a centralized structure where one electric spark influences all the segments. This same process is perfecting itself in the life of the state, as political structures base themselves ever more obviously

Figure 2. [Karlheinz Martin,] *From Morn to Midnight* (Ilag-Film).

on the power structure of private business. Ford, Lenin, and Mussolini all utilize the same system of constructive assembly, no matter how their subject matter may differ. And if at the same time a new cult of hero worship should take root, it is merely an extension of the mechanization of life into emotional life. The glorification of the leader personality is always a manifestation of a certain dependency on the part of the masses. This emphasis on the deliberate element of the soul is taking on a perceptible historical significance. There have been countless attempts to consciously change the course of history since the beginning of the century. Perhaps world war is the monstrous manifestation of this soul; perhaps the soul's toxic wastes have been incinerated in war's terrible crucible; perhaps the war extracted its poison from this excessive Will. Time will tell.

1

ART

The expressionists' initial battle cries ring out: Impressionism conveys photographic realism, tinged with sentimentality (in varying degrees of delicacy), and decorated with appeal (in varying degrees of talent). Precisely this represents a decline into conventionality. The world of the practical man is a characterless means of communication: between the natural object and the art object there exists an unbridgeable vacuum.

For the artist, everyday reality is coincidental. The natural object is created anew in the realm of art, without obligation to its original form. Similarity, when viewed in this light, is an extra-artistic term. Henri Matisse, in his 1908 "Notes of a Painter", strove to interpret the intellectual process thus: "From the standpoint of subjectivity, we have seen the thought, or nature as viewed through temperament, replaced by the theory of the equivalent or the symbol. We formulate the rule that the sensibilities and conditions of the soul, which are called forth by a certain process, impart signs or graphic equivalents to the artist, by which he is able to reproduce the sensibilities and conditions of the soul, without the necessity of providing a copy of the actual spectacle".

No copy of the actual spectacle. Thereon lies the emphasis. The artist takes in nondescript data, which he allows to take shape through his creative activity. Expressionism does not represent the object's tangible reality: it is concerned with a fundamentally different plane of existence. The artistic world is pushed back into the consciousness of the artist, who then articulates his subjectivity with an absoluteness that wrests all subject matter from it – that renders it empty. But it is the distinguishing characteristic of art that that which is most personal to the artist must be strictly objective – otherwise his art is false. Purely aesthetic conditions determine whether a seemingly straight line changes course when an artist is creating a photograph, or whether a group of words or series of sounds is antithetical to regular speech.

The important thing is to recognize that we are dealing with the artist's necessary state of being. If this condition is lacking, we are left with an empty formalism that cannot get beyond anemic, decorative attractions.

LITERATURE

As we consider Expressionism's impact on literature, it will become apparent to what extent Expressionism is a general state of mind, rather than a special case in the visual arts.

Many have smiled at the broken syntax of modern poets. August Stramm, who died in the war, published verses in which isolated, melodious, strongly meaningful words supported the lyrical texture: they were labeled the ravings of a lunatic. [Carl] Sternheim's pronoun-free, newly-constructed dramatic phrases, and Georg Kaiser's bold word architecture have been regarded as talented "aestheticism" at best.

But the recognition that spoken expression in art takes place on another level than that of communication through words as they are commonly spoken – that a completely new complex of laws and possibilities comes alive – has indeed become accepted by the general public. Georg Kaiser's *From Morn to Midnight* stands henceforth as the representative work of an era. What was once considered absurdist diction has now been legitimized as an artistic constraint. Kaiser portrays a man's attempt to leap from a dull bank cashier's existence to the big wide world. He ends with a revolver shot. So that we may be made keenly aware of the novelty of this, let us consider how an embezzler's suicide would have transpired in an impressionist drama. It would take place in some quiet corner and involve ironic or accusatory self-mutilation; a face would be turned up toward heaven, with one eye on Browning. Georg Kaiser's cashier, however, stands in the Salvation Army Hall of Repentance, left hand …

Cashier

(*Feeling with his left hand in his breast pocket, grasps with his right a trumpet, and blows a fanfare toward the lamp*):

Ah! – Discovered. Scorned in the snow this morning – welcomed now in the tangled wires. I salute you. (*Trumpet.*) The road is behind me. Panting, I climb the steep curves that lead upward. My forces are spent. I've spared myself nothing. I've made the path hard where it might have been easy. This morning in the snow when we met, you and I, you should have been more pressing in your invitation. One spark of enlightenment would have helped me and spared me all trouble. It doesn't take much of a brain to see that – Why did I hesitate? Why take the road? Whither am I bound? From first to last you sit there, naked bone. From morn to midnight, I rage in a circle … and now your beckoning finger points the way … whither? (*He shoots the answer into his breast, the trumpet blast fading out on his lips*) [English translation by Ashley Dukes. New York: Brentano's Publishers 1922].

This excerpt from a thoroughly formalized world would be a caricature if integrated into our everyday reality. The drama's concept, meaning

Figure 3. [Robert Neppach,] design for Ernst Toller's play *Transfiguration*.

and locution make up a unique world which, when compared with reality, seems no less contorted and arbitrary than an expressionist landscape. This man, who turns his face toward the lamp, parodying his readiness for death with a grotesque musical instrument, who lets the stages of his life roll over him in fragments, accentuating them with abrupt trumpet blasts, would be incomprehensible, even laughable, in a world arranged psychologically. But the structure of this work organizes his loops, reductions, and fragmentations into a prepared mental visual space: and thus this atonal sally to the great god of the Salvation Army is portrayed no less logically than that moody suicide in the Impressionist scenery.

Kaiser's work stands at a crossroads. From a distance, it seems to deal with the struggle between the two generations; introspection and structured life fight their final duel, sparks flying. If the expressionist speech structure falls short of clear realization, this can be traced back to the attitude of direct speech in drama, which tries to distance itself from formative principle, aligning itself to the very end with the natural object. Intellectual attitude in poetry is completely transparent, since it essentially stands outside of contact with reality as we know it, attempting to be nothing more than a literary creation. Kasimir Edschmid, the most adept expressionist in Germany, describes the attitude of the expressionist artist in a popular tone. "He doesn't see, he looks. He doesn't describe, he experiences. He doesn't reproduce, he creates. He doesn't take, he seeks. The chain of facts no longer exists: factories, houses, sickness, whores, screaming and hunger. Now we have visions of those things. Facts have a meaning only insofar as the hand of the artist reaches through them to grasp for what stands behind him." Though these words are quite generic, they do capture the tone of the sentiment. The fundamental disinterestedness between natural object and art object must be expressed in expressionist poetry – if there is even any other kind. Johannes R. Becher creates a "Japanese General":

> A visage broad spattered in bright day
> Where among lotuses bobbing barges turn.
> The zigzag eyes (. . . of a highly ranked

Decaying pit . . .) swell osseous spumes.
As though hollowed out by cartridges.

The formal elements do not grow out of psychological appeals, emotional memories, or vague experiences, but get their meaning and order from a precise, stylistic concept. There is no question of a portrait in the conventional sense of the word. A parallel to the pictorial approach is immediately evident: this poetry likewise attempts to construct the great, definitive moments of the subject's existence – whether of an intellectual or a physical nature. Slaughter, decay, battle, escape and rescue have grown into a composition in and through this face. This is not the amorphous simultaneity of futurism, which, concerned only with synchronicity, paints birth, marriage and death in one, hoping thereby to comfortably achieve a creative form. Becher's verse, on the contrary, thrives on its austerity of form. Perhaps it does not bear it effortlessly, but it willingly accepts it as its highest principle. It may easily be said that in this poem, the connecting links have simply been left off. It is only through the impact of its intrinsic attributes that a nondescript feeling is

Figure 4. [Karlheinz Martin,] *From Morn to Midnight* (Ilag-Film).

17

created, which hovers between the memory of a brightly-coloured Japanese woodcut and the typical life of a general. But the concept is not nondescript: it is created very precisely. The construction of the dynamic figure, with its reserve of vital motion, of life force, is not the result of sentimental dreams, but rather of an admittedly poetic understanding of proportion and accentuation. But here we can only verify this completeness of form, not explore it in depth. The sole purpose of the natural object is to act as an initiator. The beginning of a poem by Gottfried Benn will demonstrate how a portrait becomes visible, based on elements that are in principle foreign to the natural object:

To a Danish Girl

Herms or Charon's Ferry
or maybe a Daimler in flight
what from the stars' assembly
breathed you in deep delight,
a grove was your mother's playground,
with the south, thalassa, she grew
and alone bore you spellbound,
you, the Nordic dew –

[Translation by David Paisey. Manchester: Carcanet 2013]

What is here a means of composition is drawn from poetic consciousness itself. Temporal development, spatial depth, the heroic element of fate and the splendour of existence take shape, based not on the dimensions of the natural object, but on a concept of aesthetic awareness. It is the artist who speaks, and only the artist. It is not the world of business, it is not the world of everyday pleasantries, it is not the world of family celebrations. This kind of reality is simultaneously highly ambiguous and highly explicit. If one acknowledges the poetic world, it unfolds with compelling clarity. If one rejects it, what remains is a phantom, an echo, a word, a grimace.

The difficulty lies primarily with the belief in psychology. The highly questionable hypothesis that people understand each other because similar causes produce similar reactions is arbitrary. Though it serves only the practical purpose of classification, this assumption has secured psychology its primacy. People believe that, without having to change position, they can fit every possible level of the soul into the space of a very limited way of thinking, by means of empathy, by relating, by savouring understanding. They are not conscious of the fact that a leap is required – a nearly impossible leap in fact, into a new dimension. If the artist creates with a metaphysical purpose, his work cannot be perceived as art if he fails to change his position.

This forgoing of psychology, or any sympathy with nuance, is evident with programmatic clarity in an older novel by Carl Einstein: *Bebuquin or the Dilettantes of Wonder* [1909]. It is a work of very deliberate intellectual architecture, borne by a strong determination to personally construct reality. Its content-related determination may indicate Bebuquin's avowal to get beyond temporal and spatial continuity, and beyond definitive psychological consistency. "He went into the empty parlour: I don't want to be a copy, no influence, I want myself, I want some-thing unique from my own soul, something individual, even if it is only holes in the private air. I can't start anything with things, one thing involves all other things. It stays in flux and the infinity of a point is a horror." [Translation by Patrick Healy. Dublin: Trashface Books 2008] If the metaphysical location, so to speak, is provided here, then the novel's composition and mode of expression must be organized appropriately. Psychological empathy is dispensed with; little value is placed on colourful effects. The only important thing is the intellectual architecture, the relationship in space, the conscious direction of the dynamic. From the description comes the construction of reality according to its own laws. A circus scene. "People ignorant of each other traipsed in spoonfuls into the circus, a colossal rotunda of amazement, sat packed together and waited for Miss Euphemia. The ornaments of excited hands ran along the railings, and the globe lamps swung their milk buckets." The spatial aspect is represented according to its inner tension, with the aim of detaching meaning from the unique. The passive image of impression has become a constructive new creation. The point is not whether "passive image of impression" is a polemic phrase with no counterpart in reality. In this prose, the compositional takes precedence. Structure possessing lopsided rhythmic and dynamic qualities emerges as a programmatic challenge, which may be seen as a contextual characteristic of the attitude. This is the "mind-set" of a new generation preparing to accomplish its historical task.

VISUAL ARTS

The young generation's battlefield were art exhibits and painters' ateliers. The charge was sounded against what the great French post-impressionist Paul Signac praised as the strongest quality of his masterly predecessors: "They are becoming the glorious painters of fleeting emotions and cursory impressions". The painters surrounding Manet were of course not interested in naturalism; they were following their artistic conception. What is important to them is the essence of appearance, and that which renders it unique, transitory, irreproducible. Their pictorial methods become refined so that they might realize this. But during the transformation of that which is seen to be the essence of the appearance, history takes place. The neo-impressionists around Seurat value the harmony of the painting's components: the art object has been stripped of its natural form. They work with small, pure flecks of colour which become unified only in the eye of the viewer – though the effect is the resurrection of the natural object by pictorial means. But the most important thing to the artist is not a mood, a similarity, a reconstruction; painterly expertise is perceived as contrast and harmony.

A number of leading personalities pave the way through these fluctuations. Vincent van Gogh, exploding in metaphysical experiences, uses a colourful, gaudy palette. He knows that cosmic experiences must reject objective representation and reveal themselves only in symbols, be they agitated colour contrasts, disquieting harmonies, or outrageously animated natural shapes – something between animal and plant, heaven and hell. The dynamic energy of the objects clamours for composition: "In my café house picture I tried to express the idea that the café is a place where one can go mad or commit crimes. I tried it using the contrasts of pale pink, blood red and wine red colours, with a sweet green à la Louis XV and Veronese green, which contrasts with yellow-green and harsh green. All this expresses the atmosphere of a glowing underworld, a pale

suffering. All this expresses the darkness that has power over a sleeper."
We sense the psychological romanticism in the search for emotional
equivalents to colours, but no less strong is the demand to get beyond
mood to definitive creation. Van Gogh walks the path via literary means,
so to speak, and we can understand the aversion to him of such an avowed
and masterly painter as Paul Cezanne, who spoke of the "paintings of a
fool". Cezanne is the first father of modern art. A fanatic in a little
provincial backwater, full of bourgeois ambition, he experienced miser-
able lonely years in order to discover the "ins and outs of nature". He
condemns the impressionists. He dreams vaguely of covering both
appearance and the art object. "We must become classical again through
nature; that is, through the sensation." Classical: that which is timeless,
definitive.

He completely breaks up the natural object in the composition, in the
colourful organization of the canvas. The living, breathing wealth of
nature, elevated from the sphere of the coincidental, as a link to the
creative ordering of space. The purpose of his repeated admonition "de
réaliser" – which is not a taking out but a putting in – is to extract the
timeless and the infinite from a sensation. Cezanne's oft-cited and
oft-misused words apply here: "One should treat nature like a cylinder,
a sphere or a cone, bringing the whole into the proper perspective, so
that every side of an object or space leads to a focal point." Expressionism's artistic determination became clear through the pictorial space and
its laws. The reality of the expressionists is not the appearance shining in
the particular light of a moment, the colourful coming together of a
pictorial experience. Reality is only the space and the position of the
object in it. What arouses interest is not the tangible appeal of an object,
but the equilibrium of formal elements in space, the play of energies and
intensities.

Seen broadly, one may say that the expressionist rejects the psychological
connection between people and things. He organizes rather than explaining. How "objects" behave is determined by his metaphysical intent
rather than his psychology. He constructs his own world rather than
empathizing with one that already exists. Psychological likelihood takes

a back seat to the reality of the artistic aspect, for which outward appearances are only the data of his creative energy. Seeming proof of this is when the biographer of Pablo Picasso, that most radical of expressionists, tells us he has no psychological literature in his library.

Since much of the material can scarcely still be registered, it will be impossible to comprehensively describe the expressionist movement here. It will be prove more advantageous to demonstrate its basic tenets by means of a number of relatively accessible works.

COMPARISONS

Pablo Picasso's *Horta de Ebro* [*Houses on the Hill*, 1909] is particularly through-composed. The expressionist principle is carried out with the charming stubbornness of one who has just recently mastered the method. The only one speaking is the painter, happy with his new form of representation. These naked, plain cubes of houses are arranged in the space so that the dynamic properties of slanting planes, the hard verticals, the roofs overhanging like stratified rock, stand out clearly. A photograph would convey the true village in a more obvious psychological manner, but this pushing and shoving of the architecture, this grabbing into each other of the walls, this grouping in the space, this simultaneous taking in and giving off of movement would remain unexpressed. In these images the natural object is unimportant, and everything strives for integration. The compositional goal is the inventive new creation of a natural object, rather than an atmospheric experience.

Much more accessible, since the play of energies is achieved through decorative means rather than formative shapes, is the landscape entitled *Benz VI* [1914] by Lyonel Feininger. Here the painter clearly states what is important to him using psychological means; gradations of colour, intentional direction of the eye, layers of light. The Constructive is explained and simplified using colour effects. The impact is much more suggestive than that of Picasso's hard, self-contained painting.

The constructive intent predominates with Ferdinand Léger, whose work is very close to "abstract art". His *Card Game* [1917] does not try to

Figure 5. Pablo Picasso, *Houses on the Hill*; © 2007 ProLitteris, Zurich.

Figure 6. Lyonel Feininger, *Benz VI*; © 2007 ProLitteris, Zurich.

Colour Plate II. Walter Ruttmann, shapes from an absolute film.

Figure 7. Fernand Léger, *Card Game*; © 2007 ProLitteris, Zurich.

portray the actual situation of several card-playing men. Léger has in mind the new ordering of the elements involved in the card game: human limbs, hats, cards, movements, heads, furniture. This new ordering does not take place according to any sort of anatomical function of reality. Rather, the need is to visually portray this process of the "card game" in a series of organized movements, using geometrically clear, formal elements, so that the timelessly valid dynamics of the process leap out from the framework of a strong composition. The viewer's first impression is that the crazy comedy of the card game has fallen apart; what remains is a dramatized chaos of stereometric bodies, elevated to a level that transposes what is actually a trivial event onto mythic figures.

With the usual psychologizing – with "empathy" – we get no farther here than we would "empathizing" with Gothicism or the pictorial art of analphabetic peoples. There is far more an appeal to the authority of the intellect, which can only be trained, not made receptive via a quick explanation.

Metaphysical processes, which are much more intuitive in creations by early peoples, also play a role in this art. This explains the importance of Negro art, for example, to someone like Picasso. One would be gravely

Figure 8. Head, Congo.

mistaken to imagine that he is just playing games. Such suppositions are only useful if certain individuals have displayed a prior disposition to them.

The Negro creates not just for the sake of making art, but with a magical purpose. What emerges from under his carving knife brings his vision of the supernatural to life, and he follows traditions as ancient as the experience of art itself. What seems to us like a grimace is an expression of vivid primordial energy, distorted by our 20th-century bias. It is absurd to claim the Negro doesn't know any better. What [Heinrich] Wölfflin said of older art holds true in general: "It was capable of portraying everything that it wanted to portray." The Negroes wanted to portray nothing more than their world of figures, and with regard to it, they show maximum artistic ability. In the picture here of a head by a Congo Negro, the truly bold formation of the malleable object, the reduction of the skull to its essentials, the harnessing of animated shapes into a uniform model, all clearly voice this spiritual attitude.

If we compare Picasso's *Tête de femme* [1907] (Figure 11) with this one, the similarity of the spiritual attitude becomes evident. It's just that the Spaniard-turned-Parisian has had to adopt the intellectual disposition that was natural to the West African artist. But the handling of shapes, the reduction of elements to the static and highly-accentuated, the direction of the lines expressing movement, are all based on this distant Negro art.

The discoveries of diluvial archaeology allow for comparison with even more elementary emotions. The cave paintings and sculptures of the newer Paleolithic age (about 50,000 BC) demonstrate man's determination to subordinate the natural object to a rigidly conceived form. These red and brown painted bison are composed with a high degree of animated expression, making free use of their appearance. And the human figures of the ancient Stone Age are categorically shaped through the plasticity of their makers' Will, and unconcerned with the phenomenon in space and time.

Thus we cannot be said to be dealing with the "primitive naturalism of stone-age hunters". Still, the image of a woman reproduced here, which is an engraving on a mammoth's tooth found in the loess of Predmost near Moravia, represents a

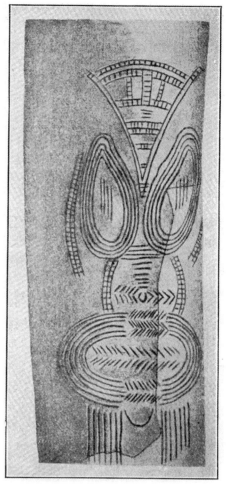

Figure 9. Diluvial engraving on a mammoth's tooth.

particularly consistent special case. The natural form of the human body is transported to a pure level of expression; it has become a composition that, in its own way, lends its haphazard appearance the clear definition of artistic creation. The visible shapes are changed into elements of the pictorial space; their static behaviour, the rhythm of their proportions, has been reduced to a common denominator, so to speak. Head, belly, body, and breasts are elements of a stylishly-considered dynamic tension; rhythmically-ordered lines lend movement to the larger spaces and establish relationships with one another. Its venerable age will doubtless preclude anyone from fancying the work an example of Stone Age snobbery – which they may do upon observing the pictured nude by Picasso (Figure 1). Picasso also strips the natural object of its casual appearance, paring it down to its significant elements. He works out the interactive relativity of the forms; he tries to clarify the incredible richness of the breathing body by making it mathematically resolute.

It is vital that we understand that the artist arrives at his radical position via tens of thousands of years of an inner drive. Here we will shrug off any potentially sarcastic remarks regarding our having finally caught up with the Negroes and prehistoric man, and leave them to their jocular originators.

The extent to which the artistic form, the compositional law, is the decisive factor in these creations, can be explained by means of comparison. People have found superficial similarities between children's drawings, pictures by the mentally ill, and the expressionists. But this "similarity" is just on the very surface; it has no soul and becomes interesting only in a quite different context.

Marc Chagall is perhaps the genius of the expressionists. Stemming from the darkest of Galician provinces, he is both total refinement and a total child of nature. His new ordering of elements has about it the persuasive logic of relentless artistic creation. His *Birth 2* [1918] is a painting with

Figure 10. Marc Chagall, *Birth II*; © 2007 ProLitteris, Zurich.

Figure 11. Pablo Picasso, *Head*; © 2007 ProLitteris, Zurich.

an unusually large number of figures, many animated people brought together through the metaphysical cry, Birth!

Aside it we will place the pencil drawing of a schizophrenic photographer, incurably insane, which he calls *Steep Path* (Figure 12). Imaginary animals and a few people. The overwhelmingly sinister impression that leaps out violently at the viewer makes these reproductions of sluggish,

Figure 12. Steep Path (lunatic's drawing).

unfettered memories from a wakeful state seem irrelevant. We merely call forth the dread that arises visibly from these instinctively-ordered imaginary beings, thereby elevating the drawing to the aesthetic sphere.

One will discern similarities between the two, and there have been attempts to devalue the expressionists with this observation. But after granting this "similarity", it is that much easier to point out the crucial dissimilarities. With Chagall, the composition is one of compelling deliberation. Each shape stands where it does of necessity, if artistic unity is to be retained. Every expression, every movement strives toward a coherent concept. Any alteration would endanger the equilibrium of the picture. The composition, a triangle with a broad base and narrow angles, is worked through, up to the falling figure in the right corner of the base, which serves as a delimitation and opposing accent. If we simply imagine this figure in another position, we will sense the hole, the emptiness, the pictorial impossibility.

All this compulsion, this commitment to form, is absent from the drawing of the lunatic. The figures do of course comply with vaguely perceived, compositional dictates. But the organization of space is coincidental; the creative thrust doesn't extend any farther than the connected groups require. It is a series of individual visions held together by a common mood, in which the elucidative ornamentation, and the individual apparitions, are simply factors. The cleverly rendered gradation of tone finally results in a unified medium, but these unifying moments arise from an inarticulate, unplanned feeling which is in principle inartistic. Any of the groups can be lifted out of the space without disturbing the impression or totality of the picture.

The painting is the form-conscious creation of an artist; the drawing is the somnambulistic, assuredly reproduced humour of an anxious sufferer of desolate and harrowing dreams.

SCULPTURE

The general idea about sculpture's purpose is that it ought to physically portray the natural object. Impressionism has already sharply amended this conventional understanding, since impressionists elevate the "real" to a maximum level of expression, creating the reality of the instant with sculptural materials. Rodin's sculpture represents this state. On the surface, it seems to give the moment monumental importance, while attempting to heighten conventional reality from within to its maximum amount of expressive potential. This need for maximal articulation helps explain why it's possible for a theme such as "The Man with the Cut-off Nose" to be perceived as a topic for sculpture.

This does not touch on the central issue. The original task of sculpture, to organize space from within, is not a critical question in the debate. This most elemental task, which is completely in line with Adolf [von] Hildebrand's *Problem of Form*, has not yet caused a Copernican revolution in the mind of the artist. The point of this revolution is to realize that the art object is not subject to the dictates of "reality", but rather that the natural object is nothing more than a hypothesis, in the Platonic sense. It is a problem that must be solved in the artistic sphere in a completely new way. Hildebrand expresses the function of the art object very felicitously when he ascertains that figures "have a much more general task than the description of an event". Impressionism forces the object to say something definitive about itself: it has no means of consciously formulating the "more general" problem, or of inducing a statement about its relationship to reality.

Expressionism in its true sense is not the solution to this problem either; it merely gives utterance to the situation which has been set in motion, the crisis in art. It is this state of a tradition in flux, of attempted forays, of bold, often desperate landing attempts, that elevates the work of Alexander Archipenko to the most fertile subject for discussion, precisely because his three-dimensional work makes the crisis obvious, rather than the solution. The organic doesn't get beyond the role of a suggestion: the problem of sculpture becomes a relationship of forms that borrow nothing more from the natural object than its static location. It is characteristic of the situation of the artist that he underscores his disengagement from the natural object to the point of paradoxy. He enhances his arsenal of plastic means which are clearly drawn from the sculptural idea, and never from the reproductive need of naïve sensualism. It is significant that a new turn of the axis of world history should bring to the surface an old – the oldest – problem of modern art history. For the principal discussion here concerns nothing less than the question posed

by Johann Heinrich Winckelmann, the originator of modern
aesthetics over two hundred
years ago. Hermann Cohen, the
great mind of contemporary philosophy, defines the role of the
idea in the foundation-laying of
the arts, thereby providing the
decisive direction in the aesthetics of Winckelmann as well as
Expressionism: "The concept of
the ideal is the cogito of aesthetics; it signifies the derivation of
art from consciousness." Out of
Archipenko's consciousness
flows the idea of the function of
sculpture, as well as those methods necessary for its realization.
He uses colours, not to paint imi-
tatively, but to place that which
is being formed in the service of
his basic concept, unencum-
bered by any equivalents in nature. Materials enter in; wood,
iron, fabrics. They are meant to
clarify the substantive effect, regardless of whether the natural
object lends itself to them. And
finally, he puts mirrors into the
malleable object, using reflections to give subtle nuances to
the spatial order. He is unconcerned whether he is driving out
the last bit of conventional reality from his works. The shapes are

Figure 13. Alexander Archipenko, Standing female figure; © 2007 ProLitteris, Zurich.

nothing more than the elementary tools of cubic composition; the relationship between parts closely corresponds to the architectural concepts of supporting and recumbent positions. Organic details are missing since they are artistically unremarkable, and a strongly individualized building structure materializes. Within its framework, the natural object – as Cohen once again formulated it – is not reproduced, but rather revealed. The most radical stage of this idea is then attained by the abstract art of the Russians, as demonstrated, for instance, in the work of [Vladimir] Tatlin. Psychologically perceivable reality is thrown off course: the graphic image is understood exclusively within the framework of its function as a creator of space, and has no sense or significance aside from that.

One may deem it a tragedy of fate that such a straightforward artistic approach must remain mired in the formulaic. This approach discounts the fact that the art object is only complete when the metaphysical resolution is completed with sensual clarity. When the structural concept is not accompanied by the richness of the once-in-a-lifetime experience, an unbridgeable gap remains. The formula may be decoratively clad on the outside, but it cannot be animated from within with the beautiful implicitness that is the object and the mark of aesthetic existence.

ARCHITECTURE

If Expressionism is understood as a manifestation of the current crisis in art, and if it requires the properties of the art object to be expressed in a revolutionary way, then architecture is, in a strange sense, outside of its legitimate jurisdiction. For the art of building has no subject in nature with which it must establish a relationship; it is the pure realization of an artistic concept, independent of any historic circumstance. It is in this sense that we can interpret the Athenaeum paradox of architecture as frozen music.

The absence of an organic model representing the battlefield of expressionist creation deprives architecture of access to the inner circle of expressionist form. For Expressionism disintegrates into nothingness if

Figure 14. Hans Poelzig, design for a Salzburg festival theater.

it has no natural object as a constant companion with which to be compared. This property is clearly in keeping with its critical nature.

Expressionism regards as its *special* task the establishment of a rhythmic relationship between shapes, which are structured according to a methodical Will, while it organizes the aesthetic space. This is however the *general* task of architecture. The formative elements of architecture represent a vital system of energies: "The column grows upward; living energies are at work in the wall; the dome rises up; and the humblest ornamental tendril possesses a subtle stirring that will soon fling itself into motion." (Wölfflin) An analogy with a natural object can only be made by force, if the ideational relationship the between floor plan and façade is dissolved, and the construction's outward appearance is viewed as an independent entity.

Hans Pölzig did just that. He sought solutions that surprisingly carry the habitus of the expressionist image over to the building. The architectural object demands to be judged from the floor plan up, its appearance the creation of an intellectual plan. Pölzig, though, builds as though the façade were the ornamental embodiment of the architectural idea, and his design for the Salzburg Festival building represents an expressionist form of the elevation, swaying in subtle harmony with the landscape. Every emphasis, every surge melds harmonically with the natural inclines and depressions of the environment. The south side consolidates the pathos of the concept of the building into a monumental front, with fantastic rows of towering arches growing up like the steps of a crown

Figure 15. Ludwig Mies van der Rohe, design for an office building;
© 2007 ProLitteris, Zurich.

into a dome, and rhythmically-organized gates expressing the overwhelming passion of the concept.

But no notion of the movement of this dynamic, wonderfully-created
building can be seen in the floor plan, which looks like a normal chamber
play theatre with traditional partitioning. Not even an important master

like Pölzig can disrupt
the decided architectural
consensus of blueprint,
application and location,
without his fantastic exuberance, his colourful
rhythm, his marvelous
execution of space and
line ultimately acting as a
monumental work of ap-
plied art.

The basic clarity of the
modern attitude toward

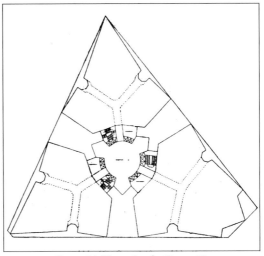

Figure 16. Floor plan for Figure 15.

life is put into far better practice in buildings which begin with the
blueprint, and conceptualize the object based on a plan whose content
is none other than the space-creating function of the building itself,
contingent on its application, location, and material. The design of an
office building by [Ludwig] Mies van der Rohe is as far removed from
decorative façade construction as it is from industrial austerity. Here the
isolated concept of function is not what upholds the construction plan;
the building's requirements are met in a civic-building sense, insofar as
intellectual attitude is concerned. The architectural imagination does not
rein itself in when facing the technical objective, but is carried along by
it to its specific achievement. Every piece of material, every shape
expresses the technical impact of the building; but it owes its existence
to a general plan which has carried the mundane objective over to an
intellectual sphere, from whence it has creatively applied every detail in
continually new concepts. The concept of the structure is clear in the
floor plan: it is a roughly equilateral triangle, forced by its location (at
the Friedrichstrasse train station in Berlin) to make intense use of the
land. The skyscraper is a rigid prism, broken into three large complexes,
and articulated by corridors that are held together by a central ring of
offices, elevators, etc. Rectangular light shafts cut in between the individual complexes, giving the building a maximal amount of daylight.
The technical austerity is overpowered by the fancifulness of the design,

which is not subjugated to the function, but rather inspires its aesthetically pure expression. This harmony of economy and intellectual attitude is represented in its material implementation: the enormous three-part prism embodies an energetic iron construction, into whose framework panes of glass have been embedded. Here the material functions as an expression of the intellectual idea, without the expedients of colourful fancies or historic echoes. Nothing remains of Expressionism but a consistency of feeling about the world, which creates the work based on artistic preconditions, without regard to conventional solutions. We can characterize this conscious avoidance of traditional experience as Expressionism, without conveying more than the natural Otherness which every distinct Will generates in daily reality.

MUSIC (by Walter Harburger)

All music is in and of itself basically expressionistic. This is true for the simplest folk song and for the most complicated fugue. Music has its own inherent relationships; the disaccord of a process not in keeping with its own rules is therefore unlikely. Music's expressive elements follow specific musical rules in their linkage to one another. I will merely invoke as an example the entire complex of the rules of harmonics: between the individual parts of a melody, or of a chordal progression, there are tonal functions such as the dominant tonic. These are things that are only comprehensible to a musical person, and which grow out of music as a form of logic that is unique to it and it only. They are intrinsic to it a priori, in a way that only the laws of geometry are intrinsic to spatial reasoning. Not dictated externally by physics, nor yet by some sort of psychological passivity, musical realities grow from out of rhythmic ones in a purely mathematical way, as complex logarithms, so that we can speak plainly of a "Geometry of (Sound) Perceptions".

Thus, expressionist music – if this is not a mere tautology – can be understood in relative terms. It is a countermovement to something that can generally best be termed musical Impressionism, in an analogy to painting and literature. Even the term "musical Impressionism" can only be understood with a grain of salt. It probably didn't occur to even the most fanatic apologist for programme music (with the possible exception of extraordinarily childish naturalistic methods such as tone painting) to take the de-musicalization of music any further than that depiction of emotional scenes which was ascribed to it. But in this psychologization, the whole of Impressionism is already present, whereas in the other arts, it had to slowly build itself up under the inspiration of massive naturalism, etc. Since music is no longer taken to consist of a complex of inner processes – we may call them emotional, as far as I'm concerned – but rather of purely musical ones; and since music is a representation, a *reproduction* of emotional processes, the entire business is pushed from the musical realm to the psychological. The musical rules of combination then only affect the means of expression, the instrument, and no longer the inner proceedings. These inner proceedings seem to the impressionist to be regulated by psychological rules; he gets them from outside the music, preferably from a programme or from the theatre. The opera, or rather that sub-variety of opera that proudly called itself "musical drama", is the hotbed of musical Impressionism. More and more, the emphasis shifts from the linear-musical (that is, that which can be expressed in the two dimensions of the sheet music) to the instrumental-colouristic. Unique sound effects take turns according to points of view, as the director of a play might carry them out acoustically. The melodic line is broken up as too absolutely musical; it disintegrates into melismatic, characteristic motifs, or alternately, expands into a "never-ending melody" [Richard Wagner] from psychological points of view. The "leitmotif" takes on the role of a dramatic figure. The further Impressionism in music differentiates itself, the more differentiated the expressive elements become. A characteristic motif of Richard Strauss, for instance, or [Claude] Debussy, often consists of the striking succession of strange harmonies. With [Arnold] Schoenberg (the Janus head between Impressionism and Expressionism), the expressive element is often one single, very complicated, consonance similar to a harmony. The style, the line, the form remains in something extra-musical: a dramatic proceeding, a theatrical event, a psychological development, whether it is a dramatic character or an emotional state of mind, or a mood or a printed programme.

Figure 17. Valeska Gert in *Kanaille*, Photo: P. Byk.

This was, to sharpen the point, about where music found itself in the first decade of the new century; it was also the decade in which the counteraction against the impressionistic wave steeled itself. And while the young people in the other arts took their inspiration, their tendencies and catch phrases from music (the catch phrase "absolute painting" was taken from "absolute music", the motto under which the pre-impressionist musicians had opposed the "expressive" music of the impressionists, naturalists and programme musicians), one experienced the paradoxical spectacle of official music's running along behind the other two arts. For the label "expressive music" has nothing to do here with expression; the expressive music of the impressionists attempted to embody the spiritual, as compared with the "play of tonally moving forms" of the older academicians ([Eduard] Hanslick).

Thus, what has prevailed later than the parallel movements in the other arts under the banner of "expressionistic music" tends, above all, toward the anti-impressionistic, anti-psychological. One strives again for the line, the breath, the purely musical-geometric form. The posture is thereby anti-lyrical, anti-sentimental, anti-romantic, since the abstract form does not lend itself to the fluidity in lyrical and other details.

However, this newer, expressionist formalism is not simply to be understood as a throwback to the academic formalism of pre-impressionist music. The "play of tonally moving forms", as seductive as it sounds, is meant as a modification of absolute "iron" forms into continually new variants of tone, melody and harmony, as the filling of eternal form receptacles with continually new contents. The forms have come down as authoritative-doctrinaire, and the revolutionary deed of Impressionism entailed exploding the architectural Procrustean bed of the strict and, since they were inflexible, antiquated forms, and replacing them with forms that were at least psychological. In this point, though, Expressionism is just as revolutionary as Impressionism. They fight together shoulder to shoulder against rigid form. Expressionism too wants to use its will to create a new form; not an extra-musical/psychological one, to be sure, but nonetheless a living one, born of "content" (if we even want to retain this confusing word). For an absolute "form" that stands opposite "content", without any relationship to it, is just as unmusical to Expressionism – and perhaps even more unmusical – as the psychologistic form of Impressionism.

The structures that expressionist music develops from within are thus, for the most part, quite free. This music begets a new kind of harmonics, new melodics. It often considers the major-minor harmonics and melodics of previous music to be an absolute structural Procrustean bed. Thus we have the often "unmusical" sounding bundles of cacophonous harmony, and the sometimes arbitrary part-writing that sound to the novice as though someone were whistling off-key. The cadence is striven for in the "line", if it is at all melodic. For the term "melodic", in the sense of major-minor tonality, seems too narrow for the wider part-writing of the so-called "atonals". But we need only think of the melodies of the Gregorian chant that grew from church tonalities, as they are still sung in Catholic churches today, or of the melodies of the Exotics, to arrive at an understanding of universal melodics. In other cases, the cadence is purely rhythmic; then we can speak of the bruitist means of expression, of the many quartal mixtures, of the diverse Dadaist and futuristic sound effects.

One further consequence leads to so-called linear counterpoint and heterophony. Since we strive to get away from classical harmony as being a more or less schematic form, and since we see the flow in the line and the part writing, we arrive at entirely free and apparently random points of intersection, even with polyphony.

The expression "atonal", which has been adopted to refer to all these efforts, is somewhat unfortunate; it too must be taken relatively. Meant here is tonality outside of the major-minor tonality (polyphonic tonality) that we are used to. It is used partially to achieve creations that approach Gregorian, antique, exotic melodies, and partially for totally new, abstract, absolute creations. Like "absolute painting" – plainly the exact parallel to "atonal music", to the uninitiated – it is a genre of creations processed outside of the formal elements of the outer world with which our eyes are familiar.

Thus, Expressionism is a problem of form. But not of form for form's sake; form as a pattern that is modified with consistently new subjects. Much more, form is expression; this form grows organically out of that which is expressed (not psychologically, but purely musically). Just as the shape of the embryo grows organically, from the fertilized egg's will to exist. Also along these lines lies the latest development's tendency to simplify and clarify. From the vast wealth of abstract creations, the most viable ones distinguish themselves, in a kind of natural selection. Their fruit touches again upon the most conventional things, the ones we're familiar with. Yet classical form, classical tonality, no longer anchored in inaccessible plaster, matures into something living – an organism, an expression of the new, from out of the spirit of music.

STAGE

Expressionist painting has enriched the world with its definitive, effective means of representation. Expressionist drawing and decorative elements have become especially manifest; a brief attendant emotion quickly and effectively transmits the pent-up energy and intensity of their forms. Provided we've recognized this, the way to the stage is clear.

It was in the fervor of revolution that Karl Heinz [Karlheinz] Martin

Figure 18. Scene from [Tairov's] *Romeo and Juliet*.

attempted to stage two little dramas by [Ernst] Toller and [Walter] Hasenclever in the *Tribüne* theatre using expressionist means. The theatre space did not try to simulate nature or suggest a fairy tale world: it was not meant to be at all psychological. What first came to light, in the harsh glare of the spotlights, was a little slice of intense unreality. Everything was merely suggested; there was a narrow bar, with high chairs and gaudy colours, rejecting any attempt at compromise with the actual experience of a bar. Martin tried to integrate the actor into this space. He stylized his gestures, he specified his exact motions; he projected the requirements of interior design onto his human body. The voice left behind the cadence of normal thought communication, arranging itself into the constructive thoughts of the stage world. What made an impact was not the scene's human emotional content; it was this well-composed transfer to a definitive world where nothing was coincidental, in comparison with which everyday reality would be a news item. And though Martin was prepared to compromise, and made the play easier through his lighting and illustrative colouration, the viewer was left with a feeling of alienation. Not even his "will to understand" could help him.

Lacking this willingness to compromise, and interested only in his concept, [Alexander] Tairov approached the Moscow stage. Just as abstract art is the consequential realization of Expressionism, so Tairov's stage abandons the representational. His theatre is not intended to achieve a mannered representation of real life as usual. Emotion, movement, and dynamism are the standard bearers of his theory. "The strength of the theatre lies in the dynamism of the stage action." The term "scenic creation" cuts through the threads tying it to reality: it establishes the theatre's distinct existence, as supported by the "emotion-filled" actor. All factors are subordinated to him, regardless of whether reality is shaken up along the way. While the naturalistic actor plays to the backdrop, Tairov demands a new creation of the set, so that the dynamism of the actor may be unleashed. "The stage must be broken up and consist of several areas of different heights. As a whole, it must represent something like an endless flight of stairs, on which the Blessed Mother strides upward." Based on these principles, Tairov staged G. K. Chesterton's metaphysical-ironic trashy novel *The Man Who Was Thursday* [Kamerny Theatre, Moscow, 1924].

The set is an "absolute" representation of the cosmopolitan city (Figure 19). Elevators tower up like skyscrapers; there's a café on the roof; slanting stairs lead to various rooms, including a cellar; and a street opens up to the left. It's overplayed by colourful shadows, cataracts of electric advertisements, a cacophony of desolate sounds, elevators rushing up and down, movements jerking diagonally, horizontally, upward. Stage floors open up, flood lights peel out groups from the darkness, people scream from every quarter; the play curves and careens through all the dimensions of the stage world.

This bare scaffolding is the perfect prerequisite for a work of art that sees its meaning in unrestrained scenic direction, in the free movement of the actors, in the unfolding of harmoniously animated groups. The simultaneity of action, the direction of movement through this geometrically stark, light- and sound-filled universe realizes the director's creative principle, without having to pay attention to the mundane.

Chesterton's entirely unromantic book, full of parodied acumen and perforated reason, demanded this cool intellectual structure, which flirts with near-mathematical aridity. Compared to it, the staging of *Romeo*

Figure 19. Set design for *The Man Who Was Thursday*, model by Alexander Vesnin.

and Juliet [1921] (Figure 18) is downright mellow and full of the south of Italy. This set does not thrust its constructive purpose forward quite as provocatively as does *Thursday*, though it is just as removed from the everyday, and strictly composed. The nature of the staircase has about it something truly unearthly and timeless: it extends between the stage and the viewer, pushing the latter down into the depths, and lifting the former up into the sphere of the ultimate, definitive composition of human suffering and understanding.

All individual forms are designed according to the basic idea, of express-ing the "dynamism" of the actor. The costume gets its objectivity not from the viewer but from the theatre. The *Three Sadducees* [Oscar Wilde: *Salomé*] are only real from the point of view of the theatre. The heavy folds of their costumes, emphasized by austere colour and light, are an

45

expression of the actors' movement; the triangular shape is their heart, the strictly divided half-oval behind them is their imagination; the sum of their appearance, their stubbornness. In Tairov's stage style, there is no coincidence: the whole, and urgency, determine everything. The mimicry of the actors presupposes acrobatic and balletic facility. "The body lends the scenic entity its plastic form. Voices and manner of speaking are meant to lend it its tonal form. There can be no coincidence in art." It is not the world of psychological experiences, stretched into a monumental format, which is confronted on-stage. Far more, it is a world with its own structure, executed in light and space from a consistent creative purpose, which arises out of artistic resolution rather than atmospheric experience.

Perhaps in this way, the spirit of theatre is accorded a maximum amount of fulfillment. However, the unity of all factors, and the robust set construction based on organic and technical elements (which only considers the expressive possibility of the theatre and completely disregards its conventional meaning), keeps the stage from its true task – of providing the audience with a heightened experience. The psychological bridge is destroyed. The viewer who sees himself reflected on the expressionist stage must be educated to do so – and there the utopia begins.

APPLIED ART

Such a radical-looking art form, with such visible formalities as Expressionism's, had the intrinsic potential of becoming fashionable. It merely had to revoke its loyalty to its basic principle and stick to its striking outward appearance, and its effect was certain. The feeling that always went along with it was effective enough to attract interest.

In this context, the figure sketches that Picasso drew for pantomimes of the "Ballets Russes" in Paris are almost too true to conviction. But he did enough to capture the organic, dance-like function of the performers that their bold oddities, their dalliance with cubist possibilities, made a strong impression. The spirit of the figure of the Manager in the ballet *Parade* is rendered with wit, taste and skill. All the attributes of global advertising, of the power of suggestiveness, of the classically "up-to-date", exist

Figure 20. Pablo Picasso, *I. Manager* figure from *Parade* ballet; © 2007 ProLitteris, Zurich.

Figure 21. Valeska Gert in
Kupplerin (*Procuress*),
Photo: S. Byk.

in this tower of architecture, instruments, and cubes. Its skyscraper-out-of-time quality is infused with no less energy than an ancient granite statue.

The music and expression of the pantomime easily accommodate themselves to the creative principle of the painter. Expressionism can manifest itself in dance groups or individual dancers. Whereas group dances leave one with the weird sensation of having witnessed living pictures and poor dancing, in the dances of Valeska Gert we see formal expressionist elements, both rewarding and influential. In *Scoundrel* [*Kanaille*] and *Procuress* [*Kupplerin*] she demonstrates the visible tendency to produce forms of movement that go beyond psychological urgency, that strive to realize something beyond human experience, that take shape beyond reality. They are sensualizations of line and space, a charming play of shapes that express the creative intent beyond their psychologically apparent meaning. Naturally these moments happen in the sensitive cadence of dance in general; and the less receptive the audience that is addressed, the more the radicalism of the form recedes. Gert surprised us with very austere forms, precisely composed. But the popular Expressionism of the "Russian Cabaret" preferred the harsh colour, the shimmering light instead; and these elements subordinated the expressionist form, relegating it to a mere general direction. The *Blauer Vogel* was quite successful.

Gifted with a fine feel for the heights to which it could climb, or the depths to which it could sink, it was expressionist enough to retain a whiff of vanguard modernity, sure enough of its audience to restrict itself to what was effective for everyone, and possessive of a healthy sense of earthy, colourful Russian folk art, which entered into a somewhat barbaric marriage with Expressionism.

In Germany, Paul Leni made a much more decisive and rigorous attempt to fashion amusing theatre out of a combination of Expressionism and vaudeville, in his *Gondel* [1924]. His expressionist sets for *The Coachman*, for instance (Figure 22), are unusually skilful at conforming to the public's taste, without sacrificing their enchanting, decorative game with spaces. A stage tableau is erected out of three people bundled up in wintry, cubist-grotesque disguises, a set with multiple broken spaces and lights, and sounds consisting of popular songs and street noise, cleverly utilizing delightful expressionist animation. The set's reduction to its simplest, clearest forms of expression, sophisticated only in their inter-sections, refractions and harmonies, is an example of the possible uses of Expressionism as applied art.

These possibilities deepen according to the absoluteness of the means applied. Typography, with its strict forms, has practically been revolu-tionized. Almost analogously to the principles of abstract art, the letters are seen exclusively as fixed variables. They are so manoeuvrable that a circus of dynamic values is opened up, which takes command of all tempos, escalations, and paradoxes. Meaning is punctuated by the words formed by the shapes. Their bigness and smallness, their crookedness and straightness, also organize their meaning into a rhythmic proportion which emphasizes the expressive, counteracts, and confirms. In the programme in figure 73 by Tristan Tzara, the discoverer of Dadaism, the printed area is strictly composed. Columns are formed by the blocks above and below, and delimited by the strong words on the right. A coquettish curve uses blocks, drawings and an arch as expressive devices to form a gracious, playful indentation. This mixture of austerity and charm lends Expressionism its value as a style.

Wherever the decorative elements of Expressionism can be applied,

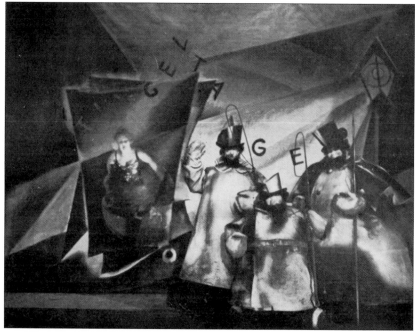

Figure 22. Paul Leni, *The Coachman*.

people appropriate them. Wallpaper patterns wander about in jagged, garish colours, blankets are embroidered with cubes and cylinders, lamp shades light up secret expressionist signs in lurid yellow and icy blue. Even furniture shapes have given up their natural arrangement in an effort to help establish a new art nouveau: it's just more tasteful than it was thirty years ago. But Expressionism's explosive power is consumed by its removal from its nature. Perhaps the most telling sign of this is that, somewhere out there in a banker's salon, an expressionist doily is surely laid out, awaiting applause. Intensely intellectual movements are only vibrant so long as they remain the strictly-guarded property of a combat-ready cohort. As soon as their tendencies stray into a broader circle, their tools lose their edge. Popularity always heralds the autumn of one's life.

2

FILM AND EXPRESSIONISM

Of all art forms, film seems to be the least like art and the most like nature. Even photography, its fundamental tool, is perceived as being basically inartistic. This is an inversion of the facts.

The art form of film is so rigid that any photographically true snapshot of reality, as it is experienced in real life, would burst its frame. The director takes his actors as far away from life as he possibly can. The more naturalistic a film seems, the more "reality" it requires – the more artificial is its construction. The fact that these creative principles operate for the most part on an unconscious level is irrelevant to our critical contemplation of it.

Consider recording a marital dispute photographically, the way it is expressed in life. The result would be a lifeless confusion of excited figures, of sneering, angry gestures. It would completely lack coherency; it would be chaotic, unorganized; it would run on to no effect.

Now the director steps in. He reduces, simplifies, organizes with an eye to "effect", arranges the dialogue, close-up, long shot, cut, extreme close-up in relation to each other – even though it might be intuitive – so that a thoroughly stylish whole emerges, with artistically-induced effects, ironies, gradations, nuances. We must admit that what has been photographed is not merely God-given daily life – rather, it has been

Figure 23. [Karl Grune,] *The Street* (Stern Film).

created anew from the ground up, according to principles that are not inherent to the object, but to the cinematographic art form.

The director encounters the limitation of creation in film's need for apparent naturalism. It cannot be denied that film strives for perfect naturalism without revealing anything about how this has been achieved. A key ingredient of the industrial nature of cinematography, this "naturalism" is the indispensible requirement for film on the whole. But we may not forget that this naturalism is, so to speak, in quotation marks; that it is a totally artificial product, that it is a style. This is why film may use any means to achieve this naturalistic result, regardless of whether they are drawn from nature or not. Thus, film stands face to face with Expressionism, in complete freedom – as long as it is not in principle contrary to nature, and as long as it renders certain qualities of natural appearance more memorable.

This is a universal condition. The world of outward appearances is not a jumble of streets, skyscrapers, whizzing automobiles, and excitable

Figure 24. Hermann Warm, design for *Caligari*.

people who appear merely as two-dimensional, multicoloured impressions. We sympathize of necessity with this throng; we experience – purely emotionally, not outwardly – the intensity of these activities. It is the mood of nature itself which is perforce felt and sympathized with, though objects are not concretely endowed with it. This psychological condition is what makes nature even possible as aesthetic material: only through it can style and attitude be effective. And this condition must be photographed right along with the film, or else a distinctly vacant air will assume the place of the naturalism.

This is where Expressionism comes in. For it is precisely the obscure perceptual nature of the environment – with its depths of emotion, sensations of movement, feelings of power, forces of intensity – which are the true stuff of its creation. The filmmaker will only reach for expressionist means, however, if he cannot hope to express with conventional means the intellectual relationships that he deems necessary for the "realistic substance" of his film. This will be most imperative when the material of the film already contains elements that are not visible in reality, indeed, where the effectiveness of the work depends upon this outlandishness and this mystery. Material that is removed from reality requires an abstract means of expression.

Due to its limitations, expressionistic film will always be a compromise. It is a superficial attempt, if one may say so, which tries not to frighten people off, and which values a friendly relationship with even the most naïve viewer. But even in this diluted form, its original power is still evident; and it is effective, in a revolutionary enough sort of way.

SET DESIGN

Just as Expressionism reached clear formulation in the visual arts, its use in film was also inspired by a painter. The process that led to the development of *Caligari* was described to me most vividly.

The manuscript had been completed by the authors Carl Mayer and Hanns Janowitz, and it was lying in a file cabinet. One day, the set designer, who had become interested in the material, arrived with drafts. They were expressionist sketches. The directors of Decla boldly gave their OK. Robert Wiene was called in to give it a try. It was agreed that, in case the first scenes failed to convey the desired effect, they would go at

Figure 25. [Robert Wiene,] *The Cabinet of Dr. Caligari* (Ufa-Decla film).

it from the opposite direction. The experiment succeeded. The film was completed.

The work with large spaces, the simplification of details, the emphasis on making the objects' leading lines as striking as possible, is in keeping with the character of expressionist sets. One must keep in mind here that the contour of every stage set leads the eye, and that the emotional effect of the set is critically determined by this direction. Expressionist architecture arises less from visual verisimilitude than from the strong sensation of shapes which have adopted the principles of expressionist painting. In particular, it offers a useful point of departure for articulating the harmony of movement and the power of aspiration. You can get down to the soul's most elementary processes.

It is a simple law of psychological aesthetics that out of empathy with shapes, precisely analogous aspirations arise in the soul. A straight line leads the emotions differently than a slanted one; bewildering curves have different emotional correlations than harmoniously gliding lines; that which is rapid and choppy, and rises and falls abruptly, calls forth different emotional responses than the blended architecture of a modern city silhouette.

Expressionist film set design is based on these possibilities. It foregoes precise details in order to replicate the constructive forms of a natural object. It doesn't matter to it whether or not a prison cell looks how one normally looks. It utilizes lines, abbreviations, and escalations in order to work out the sinister, agonizing feeling of a prison compositionally. It can lead the human eye along the wildest group of shapes, and it will achieve the desired effect, regardless of how similar to nature it is. Primarily, though, it conveys a basic "attitude" to the viewer.

This is an immensely important process. The viewer arrives in the cinema a normal, everyday person. In the instant that an image appears on-screen, he receives the point of view that will serve as a primary emotion, accompanying and conditioning all his impressions of the evening. The expressionist set automatically pulls him back from the everyday, lifts him into the sphere that is the living condition of the film being projected, and sets up the preconditions that make psychological comprehension possible. However, the premise always exists that the set designer remain cognizant of the effect that his forms have, that he judge the harmony between architecture and mood correctly, that he know how to bring contradictions into equilibrium. A street can be a bleak stretch, with vehicles and houses to the right and to the left. But it can also be a dark, broken patch, surrounded by steeply towering silhouettes, full of frantic lights and shadowy, blurred figures. One image can be just as clearly extracted as the other, if only the decisive factor in set design – the emotional logic – is ensured. This is vital, for Expressionism is forced here into psychological understanding. When radical intellectual attitudes and normally-attuned viewers are tossed in together, this kind of tactful compromise is always called for.

TECHNOLOGY

Between film and "life", there is technology. The process that the camera operator undertakes in the studio is responsive to the subjective Will of

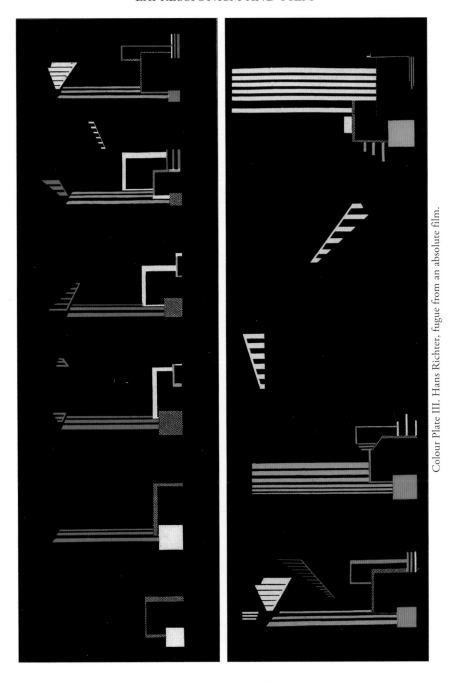

Colour Plate III. Hans Richter, fugue from an absolute film.

the director vis-a-vis the lighting, scenery, and bearing of the actors. The photographic apparatus itself contains the potential for the profound stylization of reality, which the human eye cannot capture.

Thus the possibility of getting at the film image from the subjective, creative side develops in two directions. Lighting, scenery, and acting are subject to certain creative guidelines, as are the technical possibilities of the camera. It is widely known today that the cameraman can perform "tricks", that he can speed up and slow down movements, that he has the ability to alter the relationships and elements of appearance.

The "absolute" film proves to which extent the technology of cinematography can become a creative principle. In particular, the Frenchmen [Fernand] Léger and [Francis] Picabia have rendered the camera independent, so to speak, deriving effects from the logically-organized gimmicks of the apparatus itself.

The indispensability of technology determines the stylistic nature of cinematography itself. It makes a difference whether a photographer snaps a shot of an occurrence on the street, or a film camera operator shoots the prepared action, set up to artistically simulate reality through the use of sets, lighting effects, and actors. Preparation, artistry, action: all of them are gateways to the subjectively creative Will. The technical medium is the fundamental antithesis to the naturalistic perception of film, and it is even stronger than the filmmakers intended. Behind people's backs, as it were, technology forces the purposeful composition of the spectacle.

CAMERA

The technician calls the entire range of technical possibilities for the stylization of the camera "tricks". In general, "trick photography" entails the mobilization of the technical subjectivity of the film apparatus. When the cameraman films more slowly than necessary for normal reproduction, fast movement appears on the screen – guaranteed to lead to merriment. Similarly, fast filming creates unnaturally slow movement.

Figure 26. Nikolaus Braun, light stage.

Carried out to their scientifically logical conclusion, these qualities have come to be known independently as fast and slow motion. By means of a tremendous acceleration of the sequence of images, a film is formed of such slow motion that details of very fast movements such as those in dance, boxing matches, or running can be scientifically observed. The stages of industrial labour can be registered cinematographically as an aid to managerial science.

The potential for acceleration and deceleration of movement presents a real challenge to the stylization of dynamic relationships. Other transformations take place here as well: by filming backwards, the camera can reverse a series of events, so that a coat thrown onto a hook visibly jumps back into the hand of the thrower, or a lit match hops back into the box as an intact piece of wood. The camera can create the inherent motion of bodies through its ability to pivot in all directions, giving the effect of a fevered dream. The "blend", the photographing over one another of various realities, transforms images into one another. The lens can be purposely unclear, it can make only one particular detail clear, or it can dissolve a landscape into the distance.

59

Beyond the shot, a whole wealth of possibilities is afforded by the technical post-production process. By leaving one part of the image blank while shooting, it is possible to copy another scene later into the empty space. This process can of course also take place during filming. One can lay two negatives over one another to achieve certain effects. This superimposition also makes it possible to place disproportionately small or large elements into a normal environment.

The spontaneous applause earned by the image of a bustling metropolis in the Ufa film *Ways to Strength and Beauty* [*Wege zu Kraft und Schönheit*, dir. Wilhelm Prager, 1925] was characteristic. The technical tools which the camera uses here are on a par with those of architecture. The image is certainly not just a replica of a day in the city. It is a positively artistic creation whose reality lies in the powerful working out of its creative concept. Any "similarity" to the real thing is not done justice. Various scenes are copied in and synchronized; the invisible but generally discerned intensity of motion on a city street is conveyed through purely photographic means.

The creative stylistic energy that lies in the camera itself has not yet been fully developed. The cheery French absolute films that overwhelmingly live from it are charming indicators of such energy – though to be sure, there are a couple of unusually clever heads behind them.

LIGHTING

Modern cinematography has nearly stopped using sunlight as a light source. It is difficult or impossible to regulate, whereas artificial light allows for subjective, highly graduated photography. Artificial studio lighting is making continual progress.

Not only painting uses light as a creator of space; it was used deliberately on Max Reinhardt's stage. Reinhardt's staging of [Johannes Reinhard] Sorge's *The Beggar* built upon the space-creating impression of light by eliminating the normal set. This tendency, still substantially effective in Tairov's work, found its radical formulation in Nikolaus Braun's "light stage". (Figure 26)

Figure 27. [Paul Leni,] *Waxworks* [Leni-Film Ufa].

The spatial relationships, arranged into extraordinarily simple surfaces with an eye to the most basic lines of motion, appear to consist only of pillars of light. The shapes must create themselves anew according to the placement of the light, its direction and strength. When some spaces light up, others recede in parallel, so that with the regulation of the light source, a new view of the stage fluidly appears. "Light is an eminently moveable, highly suggestive material of inexhaustible possibilities. One attempts to enhance the plastic and spatial effect of bodies and space through the analogous application of light. Through light, bodies' existing limitations can be eliminated or sharply differentiated." (Braun)

It is the differentiability of light sources that gives them their creative power in cinematography. Lighting instruments, as well as the degree and actinic effect of the light source, are stylizing factors of the first degree. If the light source is placed below the framework of the space (so to speak), certain parts of the image are given garish accents and sharp shadows. This exposure value renders some parts graphic and allows others to recede, scatters some lines, and shortens others. Depending on its direction, the light makes some objects physically tangible, while others seem pushed out of the space and disappear into the background. The diffuse light of mercury vapor lamps renders objects soft and shadowless; the undivided beams of large floodlights provide harsh, brash illumination. These are "effects" that articulate the space with angular plasticity.

Anyone who sees an image from an expressionist film realizes how much the forms are shaped by light. Oppressive lines transform smoothly into the overall image; light subordinates them or gives them increased emphasis. The light lays its malleable power over surfaces; it underscores the jaggedness and energy of the lines; it emphasizes or weakens the shapes, it gives them strong inner mobility. More adaptable than the set, it very clearly places accents which heighten the organization of space, according to the artist's intent.

Light breathed soul into expressionist films. The "lamp alignment" was perhaps the most challenging thing about them. And it's a permanent legacy of expressionist films that they have elevated the mobility and space-shaping power of light to a certain level of lucidity.

3

EXPRESSIONIST FILM

Expressionist film did not appear disconnectedly or coincidentally in Germany. Rather, the certain disposition of the era provided fertile ground on which its inspirations could fall.

Taken historically, the time around 1919 was the richest soil in which Expressionism could grow and become effective for a wider audience. The strong deliberateness of the expressionist attitude, its constructive nature, make it a particularly fitting means of expression for intellectual circles concerned with strong concepts, reorganization, reshaping. Coupled with this is its revolutionary ornamental appearance, which stands opposed to everything conventional, and therefore conforms easily to any revolutionary agenda.

It is essential, however, to repeatedly point out that what is definitive about an art object is its inner concept; its exterior is only its manifestation, coincidental and seductive. Expressionism was appropriate for expressing the mood of the time, which called inwardly for the new construction of a theoretical concept, while outwardly renouncing the conventional. This intellectual disposition led Russia to give Expressionism its stamp of approval as the official art form of its first stormy years.

It would be very easy to write a discourse on Bolshevism and Expressionism. But even if we wish to avoid this, we should keep in mind that a certain sense of the world – which culminated in a radical reshaping of the earth, while consciously rejecting organic restructuring – found the predestined manifestation of its intellect in Expressionism. Thus the boldest, doctrinally most exaggerated and abstract forms of Expression-ism were presented to the Russian public at large. All official art that was disseminated for propaganda purposes marched in its uniform. Count-less busts of Marx and Lenin claimed to be expressionist statues, with stage and literature falling into step.

Expressionist film can thank this existential feeling, the expression of which was naturally much more watered-down in the rest of Europe, for its presence. In the course of normal times, artists would not have made such suggestions, nor would industrialists have given their approval. But the disposition was universally tangible. It is significant that the first German expressionist film was a worldwide success, though much of that may have been due to its novelty. The extent to which this novelty was received is best characterized by the French language's adoption of the term "Caligarisme", which is used to express a particular intellectual attitude found in the film.

The history of the expressionist film in Germany is that of a series of repeats. Its beginning has never been surpassed. With improved technol-ogy, some forms have become more attractive and more effective, but this always involves a mere shading of the façade, while the blueprint remains unchanged. The attitude toward life has created a radical new form only with the "absolute" film. Expressionist film is a mere episode, perhaps valuable for having enriched us, but unproductive, since it failed to reach a level of universally provocative and transformative importance. *Caligari* struck a chord. Its successors have not managed to resonate more richly or more powerfully.

CALIGARI

The primal energy with which all this film's elements interact, the atmosphere of risk, and the allure of surprise, provide its élan. A feverish dream is consciously integrated into an artistic sphere that relies on completely new, untried methods. The film itself seemed like a fever dream, undergoing its premiere at a wild time. Dark streets, the echoing barks of republican troop commandoes, the shrill cries of street orators. Behind the scenes, a city district plunged into darkness, occupied by

64

radical agitators; the rattle of rifles, the clanging chains of soldiers, shots from rooftops and hand grenades …

A little North German town, overcast, angular, and yet legendary. Life goes on with stark, clockwork precision, pulsing from inside the self-important city bureaucracy, pulsing from the periphery of well-to-do patrician houses and through the little hovels of tradesmen, back to the venerable city hall. A cry goes through the night: Murder! It runs through the crooked streets: Murder! Like a preposterous threatening phantom, dreary and bloody in this respectable, tidy world: Murder! A stab with a long, thin instrument, plunged through the jugular in an instant – Come look! A tiny incision, nearly bloodless.

Murmuring coagulates like a blood clot. A breath of fresh air: outside town at the funfair, where twisted structures rend the air, a carousel turns on a tilted surface. There's a stall, eerie, buffeted by the wind: the cabinet of Dr. Caligari. Bent over, his long coat flapping around him, made taller by a dark top hat, his penetrating, unfathomable eyes clouded over, old Caligari extols the wonders of his somnambulist. Sunk in a mysterious sleep, a thin, wide-eyed black phantom in a tight-fitting leotard, wedged into a narrow box, Cesare arises as though drawn by a magnet; from out of his mouth come, heavily and befogged, words from a dream, words from a distance, words from the future. One of two friends in love with the same comely girl asks Cesare a question and hears that he will die in twenty-four hours. His derisive laughter is swollen with fear; his confidence is already shattered. And next morning, the boy lies pale in his bed, having bled to death from a tiny hole in his carotid artery.

The gentle girl disappears, abducted by a dark phantom that carries her over barren, towering walls and past pointed, slanting roofs. Murder is everywhere. Murder gleams from wide, feverish eyes. Murder sweeps its dark purple mantle over the roofs of the little town.

Only one person, the friend, suspects anything of the black phantom's blood thirst, and of the blood lust of the old white-haired, inscrutably smiling Caligari. And at night, when the whole town knows bloodthirstiness is afoot, the friend steals to the crate containing the demon.

Figure 28. [Robert Wiene,] *The Cabinet of Dr. Caligari* (Ufa-Decla film).

Sphinx-like, seemingly half asleep, old Caligari crouches next to it. The friend opens the crate: Cesare rests in his wooden prison, his sore, ghostly eyes shut.

And now, a surge, a scream rolls in: Murder! Murder! And the murderer is here, the murderer has been caught: it's the dark ghost from the stall of Doctor Caligari. Stupefied, the friend bolts to the crate, lifts up the phantom – a scrawny, lifeless dummy! Where is Caligari? The world is reeling, buildings tilt, the clouds hover close to earth, tree branches strike at the sky like flames: where is Caligari?

A big brick house! There's Caligari! Banners flash like lightning across the horizon: Caligari! Caligari! The carousel of the city is in a frenzy, murder and blood are in a frenzy, raging swooning humanity with top hats and fluttering coats – a black, dark spot – Caligari – there he is, surrounded by a crowd – Caligari – being helped by unsuspecting people –

When the friend comes to, a straitjacket has been fastened around him.

Figure 29. [Robert Wiene,] *The Cabinet of Dr. Caligari* (Ufa-Decla film).

A professor in his old-fashioned frock-coat bends over him matter-of-factly, not without benevolence; his learned head is bent earnestly. Assistant doctors surround him. The insane asylum.

His face is that of Doctor Caligari.

This story, which takes place in the darkness of the soul, is rendered concrete through the film's expressionist devices. To make it easy for the public to understand, it is explained within a framing device as the delusions of a madman. This is cleverly executed and thus doesn't bother us.

In the film there is a trace of poetry. This Doctor Caligari pervades the dreams of E. T. A. Hoffmann; he is the omnipresent mysterious stranger without a home or a purpose, who proffers people the devil's elixirs. He is a demon without a cause; in every gesture there's something intangibly dubious, in every bow there's a glance at the poison flask hidden in his coat pocket. Pure animalism becomes sensual in the spooky phantom; he possesses the sleepwalking surety of the moonstruck, beyond all our notions of culture: a hand, a deed, a thrust. Director Robert Wiene seeks to fit the figures intellectually into the compositional space: they are figures without psychology, actors without apparent motives, humans who are simply animated forces, the gears in their brains invisible.

Wiene attempted to fit the organic material into the technically-constructed world with which his co-workers presented him. He could not, however, go so far as to disguise the organic shapes of the actors in make-up that function quasi as part of the set. Thus two worlds meet that are constructed according to different ground rules. The organic touches on the geometrically-shaped; unification seems impossible. Wiene's direction tones down the rigidity of the discord; he discovers painterly intergradations, balanced with the emotional content of the scenes.

The set painters create with an eye to this atmosphere. The decorative effects of Expressionism are realized with great certainty. The set seems to be built upon a creative concept; light is painted on, and mysterious ornaments emphasize its character, like foreign bodies applied onto paintings. Streets buckle and seem to fall on top of one another; the dullness, the narrowness, and the decomposition of the little city are just right. Trees are fantastically striving scrubs, naked, ghostly, the visual space shredding them into pieces as though they were frozen. Little building fronts fill the space like foreign bodies, crooked stairways groan with use, unseen powers open the doors, which are essentially greedy, cavernous orifices. The primeval nature of all apparatuses and all contrivances is awakened, created in geometric shapes out of time.

But the essential emotional content of these plummeting spaces and agitated lines flows from the light, which artistically separates bright and dark; when painted on, it animates the spaces and underscores their disposition. One of the set designers, [Hermann] Warm, declared, "the filmed image must become graphic art". This propensity gives the set its inner life.

The Cabinet of Doctor Caligari discovered an effective style for Expressionism in film. And so this dark spectre embarked on a journey around the globe, bringing with it wonder, appreciation of new possibilities, and success.

FROM MORN TO MIDNIGHT

With a claim to radicalism, Karl Heinz Martin approached his first film. The topic was Kaiser's drama *Von Morgens bis Mitternacht*. The design was by Robert Neppach. Actors were Ernst Deutsch and Roma Bahn.

The script, reworked by Martin himself and Herbert Juttke, hewed strictly to the plot of the play. Only the female characters were unified into one single figure. Martin wanted to get away from the individual – the focus was on the timeless-eternal. "A Cashier", "A Girl", "A Mother" appear – no private figures.

Hungry, unshaven, greedy-eyed, the cashier sits behind his counter: he's a paltry scrap of flesh compared with the round, fattened paunchy fellow withdrawing his capital from the cash office, laughing his way through his squandered life, and sweating indulgence from every pore. And in the

Figure 30. [Karlheinz Martin,] *From Morn to Midnight* (Ilag-Film).

Figure 31. Ernst Deutsch in *From Morn to Midnight* (Ilag-Film).

background is the cashier's life: the parlour with the languishing daughter, pathetic and sentimental; her haggard, overworked mother; the ailing grandmother, scarcely a piece of mute flesh. And all the horrible uniformity of plush and straw flowers and white crocheted doilies. And the stale smell of the having been there, of the unchangeable, of the eternally same.

A lightbulb goes off in the cashier's brain. To see the world, to live, to break out, to lust, to grab for once with both hands, everywhere, somewhere. He steals; he disappears, taking the money with him. Apoplexy in the family, hoarse astonishment at the bank. And the police reach out after him with grasping, spider-like arms … but the cashier is on a pilgrimage to the good life. Somewhere, there's a flash of recognition: life is not on the surface, life must come from within. Conversation with a fantastic skeleton on a scrubby tree in the winter night, which comes back to life, stretches its branches, and clasps languidly like an octopus. Life to the full, life in all its grandeur. Vices, whores, bright lights; the cashier in a tailcoat, noble, superior, crème. The behaviour of an exuberant spendthrift, throwing money around with both hands – but the gesture is an empty one; the money remains in his coat pocket. Women coo over him, heads bow down low, soft hands caress his cheeks – a throaty laugh; is this life? Dance around the strongbox. What was blossoming becomes ragged, woman turns to death's-head. And thus, whipped by his own shadow along the edge of the abyss, he hurtles toward the steadfast engine of charity: the Salvation Army. There she stands, a girl in uniform, a slender creature removed from life, pathetic, all rough penance, all sobbed prayers on the sinner's bench. Is this life? Confession? Repenting, kneeling with wrung hands? He follows her greedily, the only merciful one, and also the one who always mocked him, in many forms – the bleak death's head. And she has already whispered his name to the police, the police burst in, with a blast of trumpets and ring-around-the-rosy prayers – a stumbling, the skull, all is death, the carefully made-up mask of life. Life? Light reflected on steel: a pressure, a flash; the semi-automatic has closed the account. What is life? A hunt, from morn to midnight, for one's soul, for the true, immortal soul. A span of dreams, between greed and finale.

Martin has powerfully worked out the intensity of the action. The figures are placed so they exhibit only a few starkly-emphasized characteristics. The rhythm of their existence has shifted to their gestures. The acting is constructed from the dynamics of the plot, rendering the scene soulless. Neppach the set designer worked in black and white; costume sketches, landscapes, interior decoration – everything is placed for linear graphic effect, according to the play of surfaces and lines, bright and dark. The path through the night, in the winter tree: a white snake squeezed onto a dark surface; and in front of it a tree, massive, branches outstretched. Hoffmann the cameraman has arranged the photography from the painter's point of view: everything comes out gray on gray. The human figures have sloughed off their organic form; they are parts, elements of the decorative ideas, they too create the visual space; they are torn apart by the patches and bands of light that are painted on them. This movement of humans who serve only as formal elements precludes the viewer's access to the film. What he sees are grimaces and contortions. He is filled with coldness, rigidity, and alienation.

The film has not been screened in Germany. It is supposed to have been a success in Japan.

GENUINE

The success of the *Caligari* film encouraged the birth of *Genuine*. What had been an experiment was meant to now come to fruition. The set was entrusted to a painter of distinction: César Klein. A wide audience was to be guaranteed by another great: actress Fern Andra.

The painter took the lead in *Genuine*. Klein's decorative Expressionism is unadulterated applied art. Ornate, grotesque Oriental rug patterns, rather than the creation of spatial elements. Something that appears charming in blooming colour is stripped of its crucial value – the only thing it has that's worthwhile – by the photography. And the mysterious harmony that was meant to result from throwing together a grotesque, solitary old man, an eccentric woman, a Negro, and a blond boy, suffered from the lead actress's naturalism, which could not be killed off.

Klein's designs couldn't alter a thing; nor could his costumes, which were a refined mixture of [Paul] Poiret's playful Orientalism: veils, florid flesh, and mystically embroidered fabrics. Nothing went together; what remained was a confused, shimmering image that failed to find support even in its subject matter. Carl Mayer wrote purposefully and with Expressionism in mind: the plot is consciously mysterious, its lines all blurred according to plan. The motivation of the figures is kept in the dark; the dramatic events are only inserted there as garish blobs of colour, creating no psychological or intellectual preconditions for comprehension.

Somewhere there's a strange bald character, baroquely elegant with crazed, veiled eyes. He lives in a little town far off at the edge of the world, isolated in a large stone building, where no soul appears. The high walls stare silently into the evening, bathed in the dread of the townsfolk. Anticipating something mysterious, they look with suspicion upon the only being that slips mornings through the heavy, seldom-opened gate: the barber. The old barber suspects nothing mysterious: he shaves the yellow cheeks of the old man with endless care; a giant Negro shows him out, discharges him; and all that remains is silence, dark and impenetrable.

One day the barber sends his dreamy young assistant Florian into the house. A young man, full of the yearnings of spring; thirsty for life and adventure, gentle of soul. The house will prove his destiny. The air of

Figure 32. [Robert Wiene,] *Genuine* (Ufa-Decla film).

the high-ceilinged, horrendously ostentatious rooms weighs heavily upon him; mysterious is the silence, a living ghost is the yellow, callow old man. And suddenly a shape emerges from out of the garishly embroidered curtains, the fishtailing shapes, the flashing lines; it's a phantom come to life – no, it's a person, a girl, sweetly mysterious, distantly yearning – on a distant planet, to judge by the way she casts up her eyes. She is the spirit of these things, without a home, without a destiny, without a meaning, and her dark eyes suck the secrets from the soul of the boy. His will fades; there exists only the touch of this skin, the scent of these hands, the sweetness of this mouth. Dream surrounds him; a dream ocean laps up over him. Blood lust is stirred up in him from somewhere; the sight of sweet, distant eyes; the sharp knife in his hand – the shaving razor in his hand! And the old man lies bleeding on the floor, his throat cut.

Once more, disorientation under wet trees, a breakdown in a bedroom, and a coming-to in the old house, which silently opens to the boy. There she loosens the mysteriously embroidered veils – distant, enticing, bar-

Figure 33. [Robert Wiene,] *Genuine* (Ufa-Decla film).

barous – with the sensual grace of a slender, brutal animal. Again a knife is opened; there's a flash, and Genuine bleeds on the floor, dark, dying, her life palely ebbing from her.

The people press in. Shy, blond, enveloped by secrets, Florian stands in a corner. His eyes see only one thing; his ears hear only one thing. There is only one word pulsating through all the rooms like a ghostly echo: Genuine. One image that excuses everything: Genuine. The beckoning of a hand that makes dagger and poison comprehensible: Genuine. One breathtaking, choking pleasure: Genuine. And dying is easy, for Genuine is dead.

The simple but powerful impulse that the poet wished to bring to life – a distant creature in a lonely house – fizzles out amongst the overgrown ornamentation. *Genuine* is a scenographic film that injures the eye more than delighting it, with its inorganic chaos. The figures remain without contours, the plot in a fog. Any attempt at direction has got lost. *Genuine* has no ground to stand on, in the reality of the everyday or in that of art. Rather than strict composition, or the reduction to sparse but moving forms to which expressionist film lends itself, an opera in a wild style has come into being. The actors seem to have been trained to be rhythmic, though no atmosphere arises that depends on them in any artistic way. And quite frankly, one keeps expecting an aria from the heroine.

Genuine is an expressionist film because Expressionism was a success. But rather than a method of composition, it became the content of the film, so to speak. With this paradoxical discrepancy, the expressionist film faded. *Genuine* was the official proof that these films do not constitute a business. The "boom" was over.

THE HOUSE ON THE MOON

Karl Heinz Martin drew his conclusions from his first film before approaching *The House on the Moon*. Concerned with reality, he wrote a script with Rudolf Leonhard which involved a complicated plot full of intoxication, lechery, and death, and which intensely mixed spirit and Earth, the study room and the bordello, mystery and reality. He sanded down corners that were too angular, made allowances for weird dispositions, mysterious undertakings, astrology and somnambulism, and sheathed figures in strange practices, considering the subject matter. Thus he substantially removed the film from daily reality, assuming he could count on the audience to cooperate when the expressive forms abandoned reality, in keeping with his material.

This calculation was false. For in attempting to even out the disharmonies between the natural appearance of the actors and the engineered quality of the representation, Martin emphasized the unreality of the proceedings, abandoning the palpable psychological relationship between the figures. Inasmuch as he takes refuge in the decorative elements – even flinging the titles in jagged, lightning curves across the screen, to make his point especially obvious – the imponderables of his artistic point of view are stronger than his will to make himself understood.

His most dangerous fallacy was to manufacture the audience's intellectual point of view by uncoupling the proceedings from normal human events. If this method is to be at all practicable, the plot must flow from the characters and not bring in new moments of convolution from

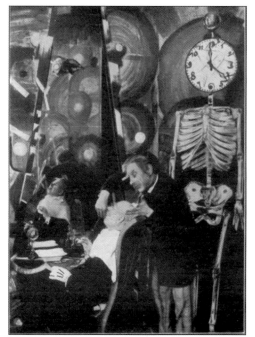

Figure 34. [Robert Wiene,] *Genuine* (Ufa-Decla film).

without. The *House on the Moon* is overgrown with scenes that are only there for the sake of being interesting, or because they bear a whisper of strangeness, making the film impossible to manage. An astronomer owns an old house, called the Moon. Strange figures lurk throughout the house's floors, from the scholar with his observatory on the roof, to an old actor and a waxworks maker à la E. T. A. Hoffmann, on down to the coal cellar and the bordello. The waxworks maker shapes a figure that resembles the astronomer's wife, which he embraces. This arouses the suspicion of unfaithfulness in the husband, who perceives only vague outlines at a window. The wife bears a daughter, Luna, who has a mysterious relationship to the moon, and sleepwalks. Conflict unfolds around her, causing the old man's ruin, death, insanity, and the destruction of the house. And above it all, the moon shines softly, mysteriously, as though it channeled destiny; its beams have infused the blood of all the inhabitants of the house with otherworldliness.

Martin has not succeeded in organizing this world which he created. The strict expressionist style of the actors, the flow of the direction – which places more importance on sharply-observed moments than on the fluency of the plot – and the tempered Expressionism of the set finally founder in a lacklustre compromise. It cannot be denied, however, that some of [Fritz] Kortner's and Leontine Kühnberg's acting, plus occasional surprising images, radiate a bit of the mystery that Martin had in mind with this contorted moon ballad.

RASKOLNIKOW (*Crime and Punishment*)

Wiene derives the expressionist flavour of his film *Raskolnikow* almost entirely from its decorative properties. He drew its national character from the material, which keeps the secretive elements alive enough, with all its mystic torpor. His actors come from Stanislavsky's ensemble; Andreyev the set designer is a typically Muscovite mixture of refinement and colourful folk art.

Dostoyevsky's novel lends itself to extreme treatment. It deals with people living on the edge of a secret, people whose waking behaviour is directed by dreams and longings; lunatics, epileptics, fanatics. These are conceptual figures which can easily be realized visually through expressionist composition, in the unreality that arises from constructive thinking. The frugal acting style emphasizes intense expression and is integrated harmoniously. This somewhat vague image gets its clear expression from Andreyev's set, which breaks up the rhythm of the vision into soft forms, keeping balance even with the disintegrated and the tattered. His is a gentle nature that loves the angular, abrupt, broken aspects of form, much as the old German painters loved the stiff arrangement of folds in the gowns of their Madonnas. It is above all the painterly stimulus which captivates him.

Figure 35. [Robert Wiene,] *Raskolnikow* (Neumann Production).

Figure 36. [Robert Wiene,] *Raskolnikow* (Neumann Production).

Raskolnikow's fate is a classic of world literature. Wiene emphasizes the great outlines of the novel; he firmly brings out the nuances of the characters' idiosyncrasies. Raskolnikow is a gentle dreamer; his fantasies are made up of sympathy, benevolence, and stifled dynamism. Caught up and surrounded as he is by dire poverty, he sees the money of an old woman pawnbroker as a symbol of the living power of gold. He beats her to death; her unsuspecting sister approaches; his axe strikes her as well. The psychoses of conscience set in; the fevered dreams of persecution, the drumbeat of fear. The fate of a strange family becomes entwined in this intellectual scenery, in which the deed is but a dictate of the darkest soul. The father is in rags, the mother gripped by the insanity of the formerly respectable; the daughter has become a harlot, to bring in money for the family. Raskolnikow loves her, and it is she who has the final word: admit it, do penance. And he confesses.

The highlight of the film is Raskolnikow's meeting with the commissioner – coincidental, a friendly visit. But muffled fear stirs in his soul – the man knows everything – and fog-like, gentle hands are placed around his throat, tight and ever tighter.

Wiene allows the action to remain in the background. He focuses on the facial expressions of the actors. The dark adventures of the soul, the pounding of the conscience, materialize. Over and over, the intellectual character of the film flows from the set. Andreyev has mastered the visual appeal of this harshly-angulated, distorted Expressionism, which always bursts with energy. The set is not harshly constructed; its light effects are very carefully balanced. With all its unreality, the set's engrossing scenic construction captures the assorted expressions of emotional states – poverty and loneliness, isolation, and the great variegation of life.

And in the great scene between Raskolnikow and the investigating judge – masterfully acted by Pavel Pavlov – the set, direction, and acting intertwine into a harmonious entity. Pavlov's expression is reduced to a couple of quick motions; his face reveals only a trace of a surreal grin that combines smoothness and likability. Adding to the strength of his expression is Raskolnikow's feverish panic, which is directed inward, so to speak. We sense how the fear squeezes his lungs, the air is forced out of them; his breathing becomes more laboured … and now, when his confession must come out, a coincidence shatters the scene. They are interrupted.

This emotional condition is transposed into an appealing visual form. Somewhere in a corner of the room is a little spider-like ornament. Raskolnikow's blood pressure rises; the spider's threads, the grasping legs of the beast, begin to move, grow bigger, feel their way along the length of the wall; it approaches, a horrible presence before the swooning man, while the judge moves to the center and assumes the fat body of the spider, grinning, motionless, radiating friendship. Although the allegory is fairly obvious, the architectural framework resolves the spider image harmoniously; the style and direction of the scene create such gradual transitions that a unified sensation results. This allegorization itself has nothing to do with Expressionism: it is evidence of how the extreme elements of the form functioned, making it capable of absorbing many different things.

It is interesting to compare Joe May's direction of a similar scene in the first part of his *Tragedy of Love* [*Tragödie der Liebe*, 1923, starring Mia May and Emil Jannings]. He is not interested in expressing metaphysical fate; he is interested in the psychological distress of the martyred man, the informal cruelty of the investigating judge. What Wiene tries to force abruptly through decorative mood, through expressionist colouration, May attempts to allow the viewer to experience, in imperceptible psychological stages. In so doing, he has directed the strongest film in recent memory.

WAXWORKS

It must be repeatedly noted that the visual deliberateness which artists use in creating a style readily captures the emotionally expressive elements of Expressionism. Paul Leni, the creator of *Waxworks*, has explored this relationship with an uncommon delicacy of feeling.

The expressionist components of *Waxworks* do not grow out of some need to adopt this position, but are rather one means of expression among many. Leni courageously and clearly transforms natural objects into shapes that anticipate the mood of the scene by directing the space and line. He inflates forms; he lets them shrink. In an Oriental scene, he squiggles them in a truly delightful and amusing fashion; in a Russian

Figure 37. Emil Jannings in *Waxworks* (Leni-Film Ufa).

segment, he polishes them in a festive, Byzantine way. And in one sinister sequence that provides a framework and a profile for Jack the Ripper, Leni shows an instinctive feeling for the kinetic energy, the tensile strength, of the expressionist scenery. Though elements of expressionist image creation turn up everywhere in the film, only the final segment merits discussion here. And yet this very short concluding statement is composed so surely, its scenes and acting directed so clearly, that it can claim its place in the short history of expressionist film.

A young poet writes three adventure stories for a show booth exhibitor. The first is the story of Harun al-Rashid and the pretty wife of a pastry baker, in which the flirtatious wife is considerably smarter than her temperamental spouse. Jannings creates the character of the bizarrely swollen caliph with baroque joviality, with masterful physicality. The second story surrounds one of the bloody adventures of Ivan the Terrible, with murder, poison and alchemists; it ends in the agitated disconnectedness of insanity. And the third simply tells the tale of the meeting of a pair of lovers with Jack the Ripper. His mask a spellbinding gaze; slow, deliberate steps; austere grandeur; all are aimed by actor Werner Krauss at pure expression. The brief, frantic chase, with Krauss's calm yet rigid face always behind two fearful, fleeing young people, ensues amidst a catastrophe of space – under walls that bend over, split up and crack; under lights that seem to pound the set into lurid pieces. Natural shape is recklessly abandoned; the bound and released mass of spaces and lines, walls and bodies, crossbeams and projections, is represented most expressionistically. It is always full of energy that must explode, animated sets heaving themselves into space, voracious openings, and the dizzying ascent of stairs.

Leni has decorated this clearly-composed set with light, as it were. This light, distilled from a thousand sources, creates feverish dreams in the space, underscores every curve, careers along broken lines, creates depths without background; it conjures up blackness on the slanting ruins that seem to stretch up out of it. He makes use of the technical possibilities of the apparatus, filming things into and over one another. This frees the motions of forms in space from their conventional ties, allowing them to ascend to a metaphysical sphere. And so confidently are means and material subordinated to the strong decorative resolve that the audience greeted these very abstract, subtle scenes with great applause.

Expressionism achieved this success by subordinating its methods to its psychological purpose. It is becoming applied art. Leni has teased this capacity from Expressionism masterfully, thereby opening up a wealth of potential for its use in film.

EXPRESSIONIST ELEMENTS IN FILM

I have implied that film seized hold of the decorative expressive qualities of Expressionism. Expressionism lent a hand whenever there was a need to express a particular kind of muted energy that was poised to spring, or whenever one strove to depict the sense of a situation beyond its outward appearance. Whether the liveliness of a cosmopolitan street or the oddness of a setting was to be rendered on a deeper level of consciousness, expressionist form was called on to provide the effect.

Film's certain ability to assimilate, to subordinate itself to a conscious, precisely recognizable, deliberate style has long been present. It deserves mention that the first consequently executed art film in Germany was, paradoxically, directed by Ernst Lubitsch: *The Wildcat* [*Die Bergkatze*, 1921], based on a script by Hanns Kräly. Lubitsch mentioned often to

Figure 38. [Paul Leni,] *Waxworks* (Leni-Film Ufa).

us that he intended to direct this comedy in a deliberately unnatural fashion, so that it was loosely associated with a grotesque. The painter Ernst Stern transformed Lubitsch's suggestions into a consistent vision. His forms parody the Balkan military milieu, swelling up into things bulbous and Montenegrin. Items like rifles are hugely distorted; everything consists of fat bellies and protruding curvatures. Expression is sought beyond reality, and the set anticipates the ironic punch line: militarism, Balkan pomp and Eastern customs. The scene reproduced here, with its curvatures and its little jagged fortress constructions, clearly

Figure 39. [Ernst Lubitsch,] *The Wildcat* (Ufa film).

demonstrates the concept. But this was an experiment, and the audience failed to accept the film's irony.

Still, the idea of the stylized film was set into motion. [Friedrich Wilhelm] Murnau, who created a clearly stylized masterpiece with Jannings in *The Last Laugh* [1924], attempted in his vampire film *Nosferatu* [1922] to create the sinister impression of a spiritual atmosphere. He used elements which were perhaps not yet consciously expressionist, but which appeared to resemble its forms. Henryk Galeen's script placed this gruesome adventure on sure footing. Overlapping visions of rats, plague ships, bloodsuckers, dark vaults, and black carts pulled by express-train horses work demonically together, removing the film from naturalistic reproduction from the very start. Murnau underscored its surreal nature, directed it with an eye toward stylized visions, and achieved the kind of horrific effect that natural forms are incapable of producing.

Stylistic elements of expressionist films have been adopted by the entire body of modern filmmaking. It can be noted that even Fritz Lang's

Figure 40. [Leopold Jessner,] *Backstairs* (Oswald Film).

Nibelungen [1924] utilizes elements of the "absolute film". Kriemhild's dream was directed by Walter Ruttmann, about whom more will be said later. The battle of the black and white birds is reduced to very simple, pure forms. There exists at best a very weak, formal similarity to natural form. The fluttering of light and dark is vaguely felt to resemble birds. Decorative space is created through nuance of colour, through rhythmically ordered movement – without a search for counterparts in the organic world. Paul Wegener also had Ruttmann's assistance with his *Living Buddhas* [*Lebende Buddhas*, 1925].

Thus we find traces of Expressionism in many films with a "literary" bent. Only think of Wegener's second *Golem* film, which grew up in this intellectual neighborhood. Wegener had a definite stylistic idea for his heavy, massive Golem, clearly reducing its gestures. The energy of the expression, curtailed to a few intense forms, already looks almost like Expressionism. And Pölzig translates this intellectual attitude into a bold and admirable set, which is based only on the flow of line, the power of physicality and the released energy of expression. Pölzig's Golem city bears no resemblance to a medieval settlement and every resemblance to a gothic dream; its distribution of mass substantiates a strongly architectural awareness of tension and restraint. The strong lines of the walls extend in strong rhythmic harmonies to towers; the precipitous spaces, the bold curves of the ducts, and the rise and fall of the lines bring the rhythmically-felt architecture into being.

The expressionist element can be seen whenever the director is aiming for something more than pure entertainment. In [Leopold] Jessner's *Backstairs* [*Hintertreppe*, 1921] there's a scene that shows a secluded moment of love in a back alley. The set is certainly not expressionist; but without Expressionism, it is unthinkable. The style in which the light is divided, splitting the visual space into abrupt, arbitrary spaces; the thrusting of the walls toward and away from one another so that all sounds are muffled; these cannot deny their parentage. And Jessner has visibly tried to transfer forms of expressionist set design to the film. The psychological expression of the gestures is truncated into intense, economical motions. He insinuates instead of letting things die away, only to have them erupt again in moments of concentration.

The architectural layout of Karl Grune's later films, especially *The Street* [*Die Strasse*, 1923] is similar. Certainly the film only appears stylized, without searching for expressionist forms. But the street scene, despite its attempt at "natural" form, tries to achieve spatial division through the uniquely expressionist dispersion of light. The sets break apart irregularly; dark shadows bore holes in the houses; bright balls of light artificially inflate the atmosphere. Thus an unreal intensity, the *feeling* of night arises, the expression of which lies beyond naturalistic means. These are elements of an artistic position which is difficult to use because of its severity, yet has enriched film as a decorative tool, through its essential expressive nuance. And that is the most important thing. Expressionism has become a tool which the modern film uses to visually invoke those effects that lie beyond the photographable. By enriching forms of expression, it has written an essential chapter on the artistic development of film in general.

Figure 41. Viking Eggeling, composition table.

4

ABSTRACT ART

The problem of the absolute is a question for metaphysics, similar to the problem the law has with general testimony. Since Kant, German philosophy has been clear about the way to the answer. With apriorism, the problem is clearly circumscribed. Judgment precedes any empirical knowledge; its claims are universal and essential. The absolute proves itself with the certainty of mathematics.

In opposition to this cognitive criticism is psychologism, which looks for a guarantee for the absolute, for the immediately provable, in the "experience", in perception. It is typical of the tenor of our times that the ranks across the entire spectrum of modern intellectualism are closing against psychologism. Mass successes such as [Oswald] Spengler's *The Decline of the West* [*Der Untergang des Abendlandes*, 1918–22], which establishes a metaphysics of history in place of a psychological theory of development, are just as characteristic of this as is the astonishing number of copies sold of an academic work like Karl Barth's *The Epistle to the Romans* [*Römerbrief*, 1922], which puts an end to "religious experience" in a most provocative and astute manner.

In the realm of art, this intellectual position used Expressionism to create an outlet for itself. What was rejected in principle was the psychological experience, the dominance of feeling. In its place stepped construction from out of the conscious, metaphysically-determined Will. But Expressionism takes on the individual forms, the visual uniqueness, of the natural object. If liberation from psychological relativity is executed radically, the last remnants of individual natural forms must be stripped

Figure 42. Vladimir Tatlin, counter relief.

away, while only the mathematical forms remain; for mathematics is the descriptive form of absoluteness.

This is the point of view of "abstract art". It rejects building its works on "lyrical caprice". Its subject is no longer the artist creating in the studio, but "collective man" as a historic form of the universal. The individual

Figure 43. Kasimir Malevich, suprematist construction.

artwork judges itself an "immortalization of the private experience of the soul".

Psychological understanding is rejected in principle. "Conventional" man stands opposite such works with no relationship to them, since they have rendered ineffective the agent which is essential to his grasp of art. The abstract artists are thus forced into the position of having to deliver a world view along with their creations.

In this problematic situation, we will need to speak more about the intentions of the artists than about aesthetic criticism. We can more readily describe and clarify the creative Will than facilitate direct acceptance of the works.

In Russia, Tatlin, the inventor of "machine art" (as it is programmatically called in Western Europe), proceeds on the assumption that there is a deliberate order to three-dimensional space. Space is unformed, "a container without dimensions" (Malevich), which only takes on shapes, definition, and order through "markers" which are built in. The relationship of these forms in space gives it tension, to use a physical term. Its "construction and scale give the space a certain tension ... by changing the markers, we change the tension in the space, which is shaped by one and the same emptiness" (El Lissitzky). This is the basic concept on which Tatlin constructs his "counter-reliefs". These are substantial surfaces and lines, whose size, form, colour, and materiality work on one another, thus producing a personal space either harmoniously or inharmoniously.

Colour Plate IV. Ludwig Meidner, design for *The Street* (Stern Film).

The Russian painter [Kazimir] Malevich remains in the second dimension. His visual world is reduced to simple mathematical planes. Light and dark, direction and expansion organize the visual space into a battlefield of motion. "The art of painting is not the ability to create a construction built on the relationship between shapes and colours or, for reasons of aesthetic taste, on the graceful beauty of the compositions; rather, it is based far more on the weight, the speed, and the direction of the movement."

Figure 44. Piet Mondrian, composition.

Piet Mondrian (Holland) finds in squares and rectangles the harmonious behaviour, the joy, of perfect spiritual harmony, equilibrium finally achieved. Concerned only with the absolute area, and rejecting the "tension" of the space, his clearly comprehensible geometric shapes, balanced in the material of the colour, tend to reduce the contrasts. Problems of universality are to be solved deliberately.

Rejection of any relationship to reality, unless it is the most private imaginary world of the artist, marks the works of Kurt Schwitters, who calls himself "Merz". No matter what our position regarding him may be, we must admit the consistency of his radicalism. "Merz" expresses an emotional state, using whichever means the artist currently deems suitable. Punch lines, the interplay of shapes, rhythmic echoes that mesh with a universal aesthetic sphere; all happen coincidentally. Technical and geometric shapes, substances, and paintings entwine with one another. There are playing cards cut from a round disk, which wears a little secondary moon on a chain, so to speak; there are spaces with superimposed lights and cam grooves. Sometimes a wheel begins to turn, coils of wire unroll, and a lock serves as a heavy accent (Figure 45). What is being represented here? A condition of the soul, a flowing of emotion; sensations of movement, antagonistic and affirmative. The disturbed equilibrium is "balanced" in space, reduced to a harmonious denominator.

Schwitters has created poetry based on the same principles, "Merz" poetry. Sound, meaning, and their accompanying sensations are rejected as being subjective components. What is universal and definitive is solely the existence of groups of letters. "The consistent poem pits letters and groups of letters against each other." (Schwitters) The poem organizes the intellectual space, as it were, through groups of letters that enter into a relationship with one another. They exist only as this elementary rhythmic complex; otherwise not. Whereas Schwitters radically exempts himself from any possibility of wandering into the sphere of conventional spoken communication, the absolute principle in the poems of Hans Arp seems more tem-

Figure 45. Kurt Schwitters, Merz picture; © 2007 ProLitteris, Zurich.

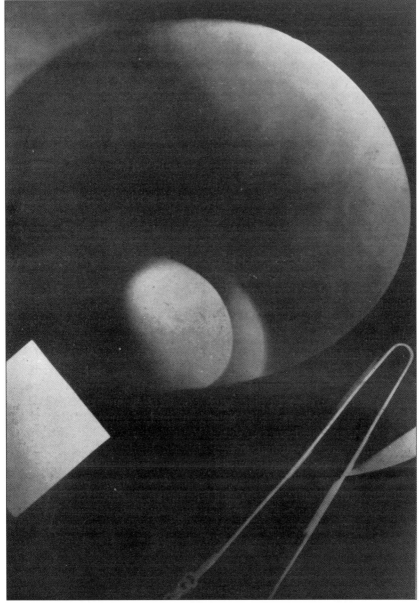

Figure 46. Man Ray, *Champs délicieux No. 1*; © 2007 ProLitteris, Zurich.

pered, and thus more nearly comprehensible – though we must warn against taking Arp's form of speech as normal communication amongst fellow men. A poem from Arp's volume *Einzahl, Mehrzahl – Rübezahl* begins:

The flattered guest.
Her rubber mallet hits the sea
Off the black general.
With golden braid they deck him out
A fifth wheel on a common grave.

Here, certainly, a surprising number of conventional elements and associations have been retained. Rhyme, rhythm and verse are taken virtually from the normal tradition. The associations of general – gold braid – mass grave are clearly reminiscent of the world war, whereas the decoration and fifth wheel are doubtless indicators of the author's criticism. The aesthetic purpose tends to involve the proportioning of certain concepts which realize the idea as formal elements. One must free oneself of middle-European preconceptions to take a position on this. Hans Richter remarks matter-of-factly: "What Arp creates to be viewed in print is certainly surprising, but then a Negro would also find his own X-ray peculiar". The question of meaning is invalid: the intention is solely to construct a universal feeling, with precisely outlined formal elements.

This manifesto was realized on film by the recently-deceased Viking Eggeling and Hans Richter. In the absolute film, history, plot, and events appear just as infrequently as do conventional people in general. With this basic disconnection from nature, everything reminiscent of the historical world in general is rejected. Elementary geometric shapes appear in relation to each other, and cerebral dramas unfold within this composition.

The Frenchmen Léger and Picabia have forged another path. They use representational and abstract forms, but remove them from their normal meaning, using them solely to express their deliberate art. With a gesture that is always amusing, they force the natural object to appear as its own parody.

The American Man Ray has resolutely taken on the task of expressing the relationships between animated shapes by using degrees of light. He takes pictures without lenses or a camera. The light reacts on a plate or paper; even the production process of the copy is controlled. The shapes come between the light source and the "portrait background", the artist

Figure 47. Hans Richter, *Rhythm 1923*.

feels their relationships, and they are worked out through gradations of
the light. The geometrically rigid shape takes on life; every nuance of
light amounts to a reinforcement or a weakening. Calling one photo

"Champs delicieux", he is able to create this feeling in a vivid way through natural means, by gradating the light – which is always effective. For, quite differently than with colour, the constructed form is "set to music" through the unfailing directability of light.

Abstract art, despite its rejection of the psychological possibilities for communication, occasionally has an effect on the public. It is just that we speak here not of an examined action, which purely absorbs the relationship between forms, but rather of an emotional process, which is sufficiently familiar to us from psychophysics. The viewer empathizes with the mathematical shapes and calls forth corresponding sensations. The procedure takes place unavoidably, subconsciously: the elementary lines and relationships between shapes, together with their movement, direct the emotion along its course, through their gradations of light, so that an emotional counter-image arises which correlates to the struggle, the harmony, and the reconciliation of those relationships between shapes. Thus the abstract work of art is unequivocally ranged into the conventional psychological proprieties of the masses. These elemental procedures get even richer colourations from the accompanying feelings that grasp the viewer as a result of memories and associations he has experienced in his concrete life.

Thus, in the final stages of abstract art as it now stands, there exists a psychological effect similar to that of traditional art. It is caused not only by the differentiated processes of the fully-developed soul, but also by the simple natural compulsion of a psychophysical connection. It is the intellectual level to which rhythm may have arisen biologically from the very beginning, so to speak – starting with the physical sensations of pulse and heartbeat, and moving through the natural sequence of primitive tasks. Whether this impoverishment of formal elements leads to an impoverishment of intellectual life cannot be deduced from the inherent properties of abstract art, but rather from its current state.

There is no denying either that this world of expression has, for the moment, proven successful in the applied arts. With applied arts, the viewer's emotional activity is reduced to a minimum: arts and crafts have in principle no world view. In the playful, rhythmically-arranged shapes of woven patterns and appliqués, we are reminded of abstract art. Its decorative charm is the first thing that impresses the viewer. And thus the paradox arises that an essentially ideological world of expression has come to pervade the mild-mannered, cheerfully superficial, colourful realm of applied arts.

VIKING EGGELING

The creator of the absolute film, Viking Eggeling, died a few months ago. I would like to note from the start that, to counter a frequent and somewhat naïve argument, he did not arrive at his simplified forms of expression due to a lack of talent. His works from an earlier period hang in great museums: I found him in many situations to be a connoisseur of remarkable taste.

Eggeling believed with fanaticism in his work. He was a man who spoke of art without sentimentality, logically, soberly, always knowing the reason why. He arrived at his form of expression in quite an experimental manner. From explorations of the relationship between form and composition, he came to the point where he expressed the forms more and more clearly. Natural objects became simpler and simpler; the harmonious character of their determinants – trees, mountains, surfaces of houses – stood out ever more exactly. Their relationship to each other, and the balance and struggle between their kinetic tendencies, became more and more exclusively the core problem. With the integrity that was his hallmark, he felt how closely daily emotions were tied to the natural object, but were beyond their aesthetic function. A mountain is not perceived as a sloping plane, but is felt to be a "mountain", with all its effective, respective traits. To him, these accompanying memories marred the purely artistic function of the shapes within the composition: he decided to peel away the representational skin and realize the mathematical purity of the sloping plane – even though there was originally a mountain behind it.

Eggeling designed composition tables for himself. They portray simple elements and their relationships to each other; elongated ellipses to small circles, upended rectangles to compact cubes, diagonals to a vertical.

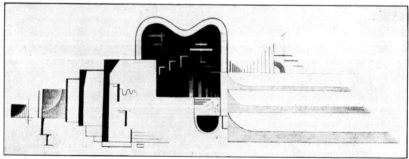

Figure 48. Viking Eggeling, *Horizontal-Vertical Mass*.

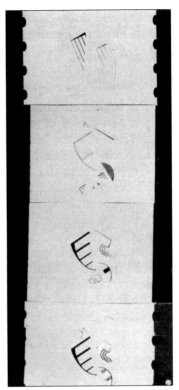

Figure 49. Viking Eggeling,
Diagonal[-Symphony].

Figure 51. Viking Eggeling,
Diagonal[-Symphony].

While overlooking these composition tables, which developed the shapes from a consciousness of their systematic common bonds, he became keenly aware of their rhythmic linkage. And since the image has no temporal dimension, he migrated to film as the vehicle for his compositional idea.

This development corresponds to his theoretical deliberation. Eggeling turns to universal intellectual behaviour; what he wants to express is man's inner motion in its simplest form. He does this by using tools removed from all romantic or sentimental memories, which are simply, specifically *there*, where formal elements enter into a dynamic relationship with other formal elements.

Hans Richter, Eggeling's companion, provides the following description of him: "While exploring the elements of the image, he found the

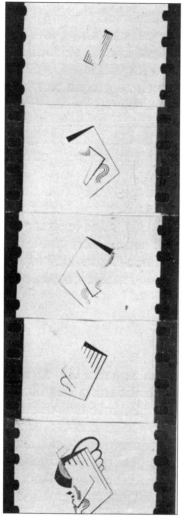

Figure 50. Viking Eggeling, *Diagonal[-Symphony]*.

fundamental principle of creation in the synthesis of the powers of attraction and repulsion, the behaviour of contrasts and analogies. He gained these experiences one after the other from the static image (that is, rhythmically). The possibility of also varying them in time led him to create the first designs for a film, in 1919." Eggeling's work is largely determined by the line. Fine rows of lines append themselves at right angles to a main body; they distend themselves, shrink into each other; they glide up and down. The way they conduct themselves can be seen not just as an imaginative game, but as corresponding to numerically-determined rhythms. Eggeling achieves great compositions through the concentration of ever more complicated forms, which correspond to polyphonically rhythmic types of behaviour. The subtlety of the intellectual composition works itself out in the refined activities of little groups of lines, in their melodically-conceived movement, in the decomposition of large shapes into one opulent, rhythmically-pulsating detail.

What must be expressed, though, is the dynamic energy of life itself, which Eggeling thought could be most clearly, most indisputably conveyed through the regular, organized movement of shapes. And the stricter, the more removed from life his film compositions became, the more he hoped to get beyond the haphazardness of the organic world to a region of definite shapes and their elementary motion, which is the fundamental behaviour of the living world.

HANS RICHTER

The logical considerations that arose from studying the operative elements of an image which led Eggeling to stabilize the absolute film also form the deliberate severity in the works of Hans Richter. The irrational is categorically eliminated: to make art is to organize the same energies that course through life, which are expressed through the relationships between the simplest shapes. He reins in the aimless dynamics of emotionalism to achieve goal-oriented configurations of highs and lows, and weaknesses and strengths, through directed variables and light. He places this work of art, which has arisen out of dynamic logic, in opposition to the psychological constructs of the day. "Instead of being satisfied to gaze at picture postcards, or the usual lovers' tableau with its well-deserved happy ending; instead of seeing the usual arrangement of legs, arms, and heads in fashionable salons and princely courts, we see only motion, organized motion – this excites us, excites opposition, excites our reflexes – and perhaps also pleasure."

Richter's film marches according to strictly logical calculations, which is not to say that the energy that inspires and serves as the substance of the logic is calculated. Its source is far more creative-intellectual. "To me, film means visual rhythm as portrayed using the tools of photo-technology; both are elements of a vision that creates by using the fundamental, regular components of our senses." It is a question of the primal rhythmic function of movement, recurring as the simplest harmony in all the manifes-

Figure 52. Hans Richter, *Rhythm 1921*.

Figure 53. Hans Richter,
Rhythm 1923.

tations of body, soul, and creation. The illustrations provide us with deeper insight into the evolution of his films. In precisely-calculated proportions, formal elements enter into the "plot" of the film. Their growth, their disappearance, their expansion, their atrophy take place in numerically-fixed tempos, removed from any arbitrariness. In fact, the film exists entirely as its visualization; it behaves like the chemical substance to its formula. The colour represents the new dimension of light; it appears only as a substantive force. No emphasis is placed on its harmonies, corresponding feelings, or decorative merits. We are not speaking here of pictures; rather, tensions are represented, which the colour can also support. The film builds itself of individual "movements" arising from a comprehensive basic concept. These themes enrich a simple relationship between shapes via new elements, resulting in contrast and harmony, struggle and resolution. The transition from a heavy shape through a medium one to a light one (or whatever we might call their equivalents, depending on their physical appearance) determines the axis of composition.

The illustration here of Richter's film only registers its main themes. Its connections and transitions cannot be graphically reproduced, since they are events in time. I shall mention once again that the colour is not used at all for its decorative function; it appears solely for its substantiality.

A pale square relates to a rectangle, whose linear proportions are harmonious. The film continues the motion of these shapes; three red parallel lines shoot up and start to move, creating a dynamic equilibrium with a pulsating thin shape below. The colours change; white takes on the leading function, passing its energy to a new shape; the bright linear movements finish in a complete harmony of white. This concludes the first theme.

The second movement continues the motion in a much more exuberant fashion. Red parallel lines of varying weights move their way toward a white square; a subtle arc superimposes a vibrating tone on it. A fast-changing movement is provided by the increase of the arc, the switch of colour, and the mutating size of the spaces. Having reached its powerful climax, it disintegrates, pulsating, into a fraught show of horizontals and verticals, whose weight and colour lend it nuance as it grows into a strong – one might say richly-orchestrated – concluding form.

These compositions are meant to objectify the energies of modern, tangibly contemporary life, as reduced to their simplest form. Whereas Eggeling primarily operates with lines, Richter makes use of spaces, with lines appearing solely as a means of balance. These forms are the absolute expression of phenomena that emerge in the play of life's energies. Psychology is entirely discarded and replaced by deliberate construction, by the active work of the intellect. "What passes today for empathy is passive helplessness in the face of that which is uncontrollable." After a hundred years, this sounds like a re-conception of Novalis's romantic sentence, "Mathematics is the life of the gods".

WALTER RUTTMANN

The discoverers of absolute film stress the scientific nature of their methods, the mathematical underpinnings of their work. Walter Ruttmann has brought his practically journalistic temperament into their circle. With him, colour is predominant, the repertoire of shapes is considerably expanded, the wavy line plays a leading role, and the tempo of movements follows momentary impulses. His films constantly jerk, surge, and swell. The motion is inexhaustible and always surprising; the viewer is so carried away by his emotions that he is not conscious of the fact that he is seeing inorganic shapes.

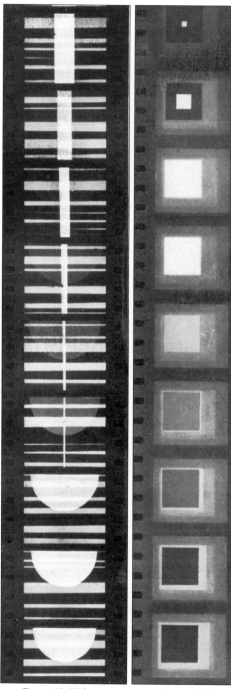

The colour is particularly exciting. Ruttmann uses an unusually rich palette, with a new mellow hue for every nuance of movement. Sentimental, sharp, happy, and cheerful gradations of colour change with the progression of curves, the lurching forward and the twitching back of his squares and rectangles. One feels that these organically swelling shapes eat each other, devour each other, charge at each other in combat, embrace each other lovingly: it's a drama of colourful shapes that automatically compels an emotional reaction. Ruttmann has attained considerable success with an industrial advertising film of this sort, which clearly demonstrates how expressive these colourfully-moving shapes are.

The strong appeal of Ruttmann's films lies in the psychological stim-

Figure 54. Walter Ruttmann, motifs.

Figure 55. Walter Ruttmann, motifs.

uli which make them continually effective. His compositions are dramatic, employing as actors geometric shapes which reverberate with a wealth of organic echoes. He does away with the strict constructive direction which others favour: his dynamics are not developed, but rather experienced. Curvy spaces vibrate in harmony, the hurtling forward of bodies surprises us, and changes in shape carry us along. Everything follows quickly; the viewer is pulled into a whirlwind of motion and integrated into an atmospheric blend of colours that never leaves him for an instant. Squares and rectangles shoot forward, multiply, disappear, turn up in unexpected points in space, and exchange energies with one another in the most astonishing fashion. A resonance with the soul is generated, as in an internal combustion engine. Then wavy motions, now gentle, now violent, overrun the image; they tear off into shapes and join together harmoniously. The colour shading, graded into the tiniest detail, trickles grace and sweetness, passion and agitation, into the viewer's heart.

Ruttmann's effect is so irresistible that he has been called upon many times to compose his kind of scene for conventional fiction films. Normally these are events of an unreal nature, beyond visibility, which must be expressed in a pictorially potent form that is apart from daily life. Ruttmann does not attempt to express the energies of life in mathematically-determined, timeless forms; he takes feeling, decorative charm, and psychological effect into his calculations. But it is precisely his flexibility regarding principles that makes him the most promising producer of absolute films, in a commercial sense. For in his films, the bridge to the world of daily experience remains intact – if not visibly, then emotionally. Such a bridge has been definitively destroyed by the others.

FERNAND LÉGER

I would like to repeat here at the onset that Léger is one of the great French painters. He is well-recognized. Léger is in principle in agreement with Eggeling and Richter, with whom he formed an alliance. His shapes serve only to realize the artist's emotional attitude. But Léger retains the

Figure 56. Fernand Léger, *Ballet mécanique*; © 2007 ProLitteris, Zurich

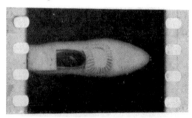

Figure 57. Fernand Léger, *Ballet mécanique*; © 2007 ProLitteris, Zurich

Figure 58. Fernand Léger, *Ballet mécanique*; © 2007 ProLitteris, Zurich

Figure 59. Fernand Léger, *Ballet mécanique*; © 2007 ProLitteris, Zurich

Figure 60. Fernand Léger, *Ballet mécanique*; © 2007 ProLitteris, Zurich

greatest freedom for himself in his choice of tools. He employs organic, technical and mathematical images: his dynamic representations do not eschew the feelings which accompany familiar objects. Thus his film builds up a tremendous world of resources that help him realize the "plot" – admittedly a composition constructed by the artist so that he may portray the dynamic behaviour of shapes. He is only interested in the intensity of motion which every form harnesses, whether it is a mathematical image or an element of daily life. "Daily life is so breathless that everything has become animated and mobile. Such a dynamic rhythm prevails that the slice of life as glimpsed from a café terrace has become a true drama, with eclectic components conflicting with and affecting one another." It is the expression of this tension, the representation of the relationships between these shapes and their tempos, which make up Léger's films.

Constructively, following his design, he proceeds from the camera's capabilities. This method of creation, via the means of the camera, is decisive. Only by virtue of it can the film be realized. "The novelized film possesses a fundamental flaw that stems from the literary background and attitude of most directors. Despite their indis-

Figure 61. Fernand Léger, *Ballet méchanique*; © 2007 ProLitteris, Zurich

Figure 62. Fernand Léger, *Ballet méchanique*; © 2007 ProLitteris, Zurich

putable talent, they are poised undecided between the script as a mere tool and the animated image as the actual objective. They constantly confuse the one with the other, and get their order backward." Léger wants to get back to the central point of departure of the film images. His film is the plastic expression of an artist carried along by the speed of modern movement, by the dynamism of cosmopolitan life. A pair of beautiful legs appears, the dream of every adolescent male, but they are fakes arranged around a control apparatus, making all sexuality look foolish. Funnels, cooking utensils, cylinders, and bottles roll across the screen, tilt over each other, rotate, arrange themselves, multiply pointlessly, and fill the space with rapid-fire movements. They appear between organic groups of moving objects, in an exploding entr'acte. Suddenly a face pops up, a pair of

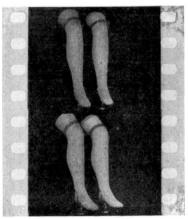

Figure 63. Fernand Léger, *Ballet méchanique*; © 2007 ProLitteris, Zurich

expressive eyes, it's something that somehow evokes feeling; and now, through the camera's tricks and the fast tempo of turning objects, it's virtually compromised, a mere object at rest, purely decorative. A pearl necklace appears, beautiful, impassive: the words "a necklace" appear in large letters underneath it. Geometric images cut across the space, rest on it, and take on colour. A straw hat can be a calming influence amidst the stampede of visions, as it lies there in its band-decorated grandeur, or can even enter into a contradictory still life with surfaces, shadows, and geometric spatial arrangements. And in a suspension of all natural laws, or like a metaphysical joke that subverts human endeavour, an old woman marches up a lane, waves amiably, reaches her goal, and suddenly starts over again, strives diligently upward, waves amiably, draws a deep breath on top, and starts over, inexhaustibly climbing, waving, is on top and then climbing again, arduously starting up, waving, …. And again, down, up, down, up, waving, smiling, happily starting over, up, down … the film sequence is repeated a dozen times over.

It is a subtle mockery of tangible, visual existence. It is also a visual demonstration of the task of abstract art, which is to reduce problematic reality to definitive forms, and to unfurl the interplay of forces as they are conceived, clear and undiluted by the adventures in daily life. What happens in the film is an expression of dynamic values. Infinity, parodied through an old woman; the turning of plates, machine parts, cubes, surfaces; the collision of ambiguous organic images, like the charming straw hat with geometric designs: this represents the same attitude as the German absolute film; it is just expressed using different means.

It is the amusing conversational tone of the Frenchman, [Alfred] Kerr's "luminous clarity of the Gauls", that gives these films their charming playful flow, without robbing them of a serious artistic attitude. The "plot" is organized around the visual allure, in order to realize the artist's ideas about organized movement. Léger feels forced into this rapidissimo of creation by the competitiveness of modern life. He fights for the victory of human creation over the monumental architectural structure of motion in daily life. It is a lost battle if one uses the same material as life itself, but a battle that can be won if one draws material from artistic consciousness, viewing daily reality only as "malleable material". Thus the metaphysical approach of Léger's film turns back to the Germans' formulation of the problem. But instead of exactly portraying relationships in motion, he shifts their expression to tangible visualization. Still, he avoids psychological ingratiation; nothing figurative or colourful exists only because it's decorative. The concept remains strictly pure. But after all, style, lightness, and charm are said to be French national traits. One can accept that or reject it. Léger's film will be entertaining in a deeper sense to anyone who might enjoy going to a big metaphysical circus.

FRANCIS PICABIA

The methods one chooses with which to fight for the course that the intellect should take vary, according to one's temperament. This Francis Picabia is a healthy he-man, with a deep antipathy to the catch phrase, or anything standing still or conventional, and with a deep sympathy for anything that destroys reality in order to keep essential metaphysical curiosity alive. A man without pathos, even his venom is conversational; he is distinguished by irony, refinement, and an intellectual subtlety that takes in every opportunity instantaneously. Setting himself no long-term goals, he welcomes everything that spoils the normal person's pleasure in reality, or that wreaks havoc, or that has a personal face. His natural role is that of the bluffer; first of all, he must rattle the bourgeois status quo. He is so in love with his methods that he sometimes loses sight of his intention and produces his eccentric gymnastics just for the thrill of the concussion. He begins, for example, with a melodramatic exhortation:

> You are all being indicted: all rise!
>   I can only talk to you if you're standing …
> You've all sat down again? All the better; then
>   you'll listen to me more attentively.

Picabia's film is also always in charge. Organic and geometric shapes are all the same to him. The dynamics of his attitude toward life translate into a madly moving vision of figures that come into play in perpetually new and surprising relationships. He is nowhere near enough of a taxonomist to be able to steer every attendant emotion, every memory of daily life, toward its own parody. All right then, they can think a lamp is a lamp, even though the image shows nothing more than a little rigid pyramid on a solid base, with a spout growing out of it. Something slanted with a few bulges, which releases peculiar tensions when it crashes into a cube. He decorated a Swedish ballet called *Relâche*, in which the entire world of shapes seems to be at work. There is a background of round forms, now light, now dark, which create multiple visual impulses; there are costumes that gradate by colour and shape, whose figures overlap. Something has come out of this decoration which resounds but is unrecognizable in the light, and expands the space beyond its natural dimensions. It is as full of motion as the spirit of ballet itself.

Certainly, he is no taxonomist. His film even has a plot; the adventures of a funeral procession. But these adventures originate in the camera: they are decelerations and accelerations that unspool in surprising increments. It is the movement itself, tied to a somehow recordable procedure, which comes up against the viewer's feeling about life. The humour is created through the memory of the normal occasion of a funeral procession, which is parodied, in a manner of speaking, across all points in time. Ideas insert themselves in between these images, splitting the dynamism of the modern sense of the world into a beam of light, so to speak. Someone wants badly to shoot something, and sooner or later gets shot himself. But is only a metaphysical gesture, for weapons are after all only bodies that to some extent create movement, and people who want to shoot are certainly comical, if one casts an eye on the whole apparatus of taking aim, searching, pointing, and firing. And woven into this is the eternal monumental rhythm of the metropolis, dissolved into sometimes abstract, sometimes organic shapes, parodying the energies of life itself. A little paper boat floats slowly over the sea of buildings in Paris. It is the fanatically-conceived melody of motion, its modulation, its accelerations and stops, which is created from the spirit and the tools of cinematography. Of all those who have created absolute films, Picabia is the least systematic and at the same time the most resolute. He can be funny in a very bourgeois way, but behind that is the parody of the joke itself. It is in fact metaphysical purpose that flares up everywhere, and if one looks over his paintings, drawings, and manifestos, one senses the distilled spirit of motion, one senses in all the somersaults the unshakable axis of this gyrating world: the belief in art.

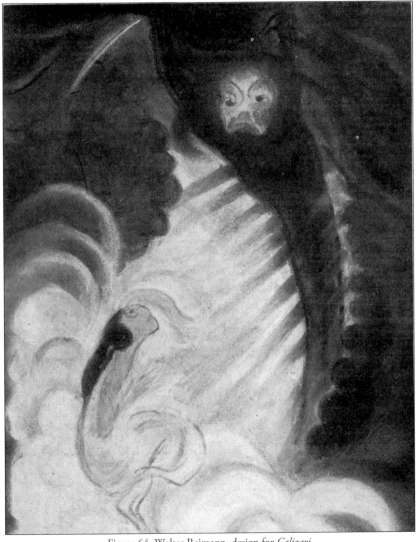

Figure 64. Walter Reimann, design for *Caligari*.

5

STYLE IN EXPRESSIONIST FILM

The expressionist film is a highly artistic organism that represents a specific shaping of reality. This form cannot be created by building expressionist sets, or theatrical modes of expression, in just any kind of film. Rather, the expressionist film is the result of a unique composition that consistently takes hold of, and expediently reshapes, all of the film's components.

To begin with, it is doubtful whether we can even speak of an expressionist film style. The term "style" generally blurs amidst the variety of individual perceptions; it can be considered a legitimization, so to speak, of a highly problematic personality. Style will be used here in the sense of an aesthetically unified expression, by which the artistic individual understands and portrays reality. Insofar as Expressionism represents a well characterized, intellectual attitude of this kind, we can refer to its style.

The failure to carry out this style causes dilettantism in film. The embarrassing sensation that *Genuine* leaves behind can be traced back to the fact that the actors act very naturalistically, but that the set designer borrows decorative elements from the most varied schools of thought, thus rendering a conglomerate that disseminates restlessness everywhere – whereas style represents harmony amid the uproar. Film does not allow actors to be reconfigured as elements of the set, any more than the stage allows it. The attempt to breathe new life into antique actors' masks did not work even for Goethe, with his performances of Terence in Weimar. And it never will succeed, for the emotional events that ultimately ensue from a stage or film performance still retain too many intellectually and psychologically splintered elements for the face, or the gesture, to sustain a unified expression. Perhaps this strict, systematic resolution is possible in ballet, which is capable of reducing the life of the moving form to a purely visual process, and can rely on the music.

But the parts must be in harmony if the film is to have an effect; and if the director's intention tends toward expressionistic representation, he must carry this form through to all its details. Where serious hindrances present themselves, he must carry out transitions, modulations, mitigations. If this inner harmony is not produced, the film disintegrates, and no contact is made with the viewer, since no tone is allowed to resonate. Expressionist elements in a film are no guarantee of style – on the contrary, such powerful explosive material easily casts the director's creative energy asunder, exploding the frame of the film beyond retrieval.

DIRECTION

The director represents the natural focal point of the film, where energies concentrate and receive guidance and a position. He is the guarantor of unity. In his hand rests the system of emphases, omissions, shadings, colourations, tempo regulations, and intonations that make the difference in the spirit and texture of the film. The director's effectiveness gives the film a unified note that goes beyond the collaboration of individual factors.

Expressionism in film represents such an expenditure of visual energy and surprise, and such a wealth of material, that the hand that organizes the elements is not particularly conspicuous. In our analysis, we will need to restrict ourselves to details that occasionally flash forth. We can merely explain the means by which the director achieves expressionist form, and the extent to which he positions them as purely decorative tools in his instrumentarium of forms.

Robert Wiene approached *Caligari* with the zeal of a man out to conquer

Figure 65. [Robert Wiene,] *Raskolnikow* (Neumann Production).

virgin territory. He tried to mitigate the discrepancy between the two pillars of film that are polar opposites: the insurmountably natural shape of the actors, and the essentially artificial form of the sets. He attempted this by getting the actors to recede into, and assimilate to, the set. But this schism, which might have sealed the film's fate, was overcome quite positively through the creative energy of Krauss and Veidt, whose acting is strong, with an eye toward the metaphysical concept. They keep the foreground in motion so strongly that the other figures can be moved back directorially into a less colourful atmosphere. Wiene gradates their transitions, and creates balance through costume and posture. *Genuine* lacks strong actors, and Wiene tries to create the unity of man and landscape, of actor and set, through equal alignment of each factor. The actors' physical posture is expressionistic; their gestures manifest vigorous movement within the space, their facial expressions strive toward the statuary, the typical. But the creative purpose is consumed by the generally chaotic style; the expression, insofar as Gronau succeeds with the individual detail, remains isolated and noncommittal on the whole.

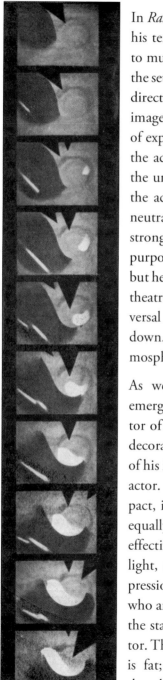

Figure 66. Walter Ruttmann, motifs.

In *Raskolnikow*, Robert Wiene once again follows his tendency to let the mood of the scene speak, to mute the actors, and to trust the superiority of the set and the impression made by the image. The director orients himself to the composed film image. He wants to achieve a maximum amount of expression with the set decoration by muffling the actor – whose corporeality is a hindrance to the uniformity of elements in the image. He has the actor omit naturalistic eruptions and seek a neutral expression, rather than veering off toward strong forms that were designed for a different purpose. Wiene's direction is accommodating, but he is also man enough to bring truly important theatrical personalities into harmony with his universal intellectual design, without watering them down. On the contrary, the generally stylish atmosphere stimulates great stylish creation.

As we evaluate methods, Karl Heinz Martin emerges at the opposite pole, as a conscious director of actors. He does not direct from inside the decorative architecture: rather, the representative of his intellectual purpose is first and foremost the actor. The art form in general must have an impact, in order to influence all aspects of the film equally. Martin is stricter than Wiene, but also less effective filmically. He rejects reliable effects; set, light, and image detail take a back seat. The expressionist Will reveals itself initially in the actors, who are elevated to a new plane of existence from the start, having become inventions of the director. The fat man is the archetype of everything that is fat; painted lights jump brightly across his shapeless body, definitively characterizing it as a pure form. The cashier has become an entirely

118

Figure 67. Werner Krauss in *Waxworks* (Leni-Film Ufa).

stylistic expression, skinny, unnaturally pale, his beard a scrawny forest, torn asunder by the light that entraps him; he is the picture of a fraud, rendered unsuccessful by a mental defect at birth. If they were arranged into the normal scheme of life, the figures would be pointless caricatures; but then the normal scheme of life is yesterday's news, like Biedermeier and the stagecoach. Their manner of representation, the way these constructed figures function, orients itself to this thoroughly artificial existence. Transitions disappear, psychological understanding recedes, one sharply accentuated moment stands firmly opposed to another; it is a battle of catchwords. And it is led by an unrelentingly potent intellectual energy that the plot shades rhythmically, so to speak, shoving people and situations into the light as required. This results in a sudden roar, then an abrupt silence: it's a directing style for which life's motion, as an extension of its intrinsic power, is the essential thing. With *The House on the Moon,* Martin's directing style has become milder. After his failed experiment, he wants to find a connection to his audience. The image's intellectual structure has not changed significantly. The figures, not architectural shapes so much as living people, still shoot off condensed experiences in a single instant; gestures appear abruptly for intensity's sake; the unreal still pushes forth definitively. The need to make the characters' behaviour understood to the audience leads Martin to allow conventionally acted moments to slip in.

However, he can't get beyond the discrepancy of having islands of manipulated bourgeois conversation embedded in expressionistically strict forms. The intellectual course of the direction remains unchanged; it's only that the means have been tempered. If he once succeeds in achieving a memorable image, the audience rebels, not understanding why this kind of expression has sneaked in, and dimly sensing the discrepancy in style. It is inherently impossible for a figure to represent a formal element one time, and a regular denizen of the familiar earth the next.

Martin knows that in pure art, the natural object can only exist as expression and form. With film, it is probably possible to catch the audience up in the moods of expressionistic scenery, but it is impossible to keep them from seeing the person next door – or in any case someone like them – in a human figure. And the more energetically Martin works out the purpose of his creative intent, the faster his film becomes ineffective.

SCRIPT

The importance of the manuscript for the film has not been at all clarified. A fundamental aesthetic analysis is lacking, and thus latitude is afforded the personal version. Without getting into specific details, we can ascertain that the intellectual coordinate system of the film, so to speak, is determined by the manuscript. The position of the formal elements is fixed in it, from the complex of scenes to the tiniest detail, the balance of intellectual developments, and the setting of the emotional tone. The director has freedom only with the individual moment, the placement of the figure and plot in the pictorial space. Even here, he is free only if he decides not to interfere with the script, which is a concern of the writer rather than the director.

Thus a normal manuscript cannot provide the basis for an expressionist film, since it is decisively influenced by psychological means. The expressionist film sets up a living space which is fundamentally different from that of the experienced world, as a precondition to its existence. This

Figure 68. [Paul Leni,] *Waxworks* (Leni-Film Ufa).

distance from everyday existence must be provided by the expressionist film script, if it is to be realized accordingly.

The means of producing these preconditions vary. Normally, Mystery imposes itself on the atmosphere of the script, since that is the easiest way to express remoteness from reality. Peculiarity is the raw material, the usual surrogate for the heightening of existence to a point at which daily experiences lose their actual tone and appear simply as Purpose, Form and Destiny.

The actual creator of the expressionistic film script, – in Germany there is only one, Carl Mayer – proceeded from this mind-set with his *Caligari* manuscript (together with Hans Janowitz). Caligari represents a fate outside the day-to-day, a feverish experience. The author legitimizes his own position to the audience by presenting it as the hallucination of a lunatic. But Mayer, for whom the term Expressionism means more than mere decoration, quickly grows out of this compromise. The material loses its mechanical bizarreness, remaining in the realm of matter-of-fact experience. It is pure poetic energy that lifts it to a metaphysical plane. Now the bourgeois loses its usual contour: the figures become forms with a compositional purpose. The external process becomes concentrated, metamorphosing into dynamic tension; the plot's sparseness allows it to dissolve into ever finer rhythmic relationships. This position gives Mayer's script its external face: he writes his sentences with an eye toward dynamic effect. His self-reliant prose conveys to the director his ideas regarding intensity. He uses repetition, reorganization of sentences, and the rhythmic arrangement of words to oblige him to adopt a kindred attitude. A scene from Mayer's script for *Sylvester: New Year's Eve* [*Sylvester: Tragödie einer Nacht*, 1924] illustrates how tension develops and the human being transforms into an intellectual figure within the filmic space:

In the pastry shop.

Light goes up slightly.

Total: Fumes. Smoke. Dim Light. The piano is tinkling.
And!
While new customers keep coming in: the waiters run
Through all the laughing and drunken noise.
And!
At the bar. The man. He works. For many.
Yet!
     Closer: Since he just settled a situation.   And he takes a
breather for a second: He looks back
at the door.   Somehow expectantly.
And!
Now!
Suddenly.   He still hails a waiter.   Then:
He leaves. Quickly. Backwards.

The artistic determination to get away from the time-bound and toward an absolute comes markedly to the fore. Lupu Pick, the director of the film, puts it purely emotionally in a foreword: "As I read the manuscript, I was moved by the immortality of the themes." The escape from psychology is also clear to the director; the sea and the metropolis take on metaphysical functions, not as the scene of the action, but as compo-

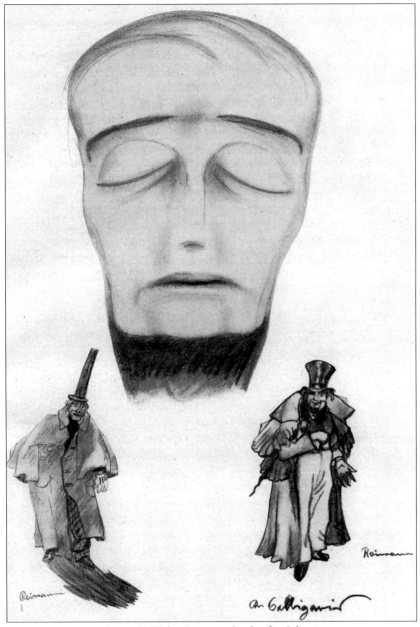

Figure 69. Walter Reimann, sketches for *Caligari*.

sitional tools. It is their task "to form the symphonic underground and background for the individual fate, thus best incorporating the fundamental idea". Pick's comments are all the more interesting since he clarifies an unusually significant process, explaining the clearly expressionistic attitude of a work through psychological means. Mayer wants to create the dynamics of a clearly conceived slice of the world, while Pick relocates its tone from the constructive to the interpretive: the rhythm is certainly the main thing, but it expresses itself in the emotional relationships of the figures. When Pick interprets the purpose of the *Lichtspiel* ["light play"] as creating "the eternal exchange of light and shadow in the spiritual relationships between people", then the two opposite worlds, dominion of movement and dominion of the soul, flow together as one. Pick took this intellectual attitude while directing the film, incorporating the metaphysical intent of the author into the stylish psychological construction of characters, while striving to achieve rhythm by including the sea and a metropolis. But a clear contradiction emerges in the form of the film. It is not absolutely necessary to choose a manuscript with an expressionistic point of view. But if a plot that relies on the rhythm of formal elements for its vital impulse is placed on a psychological-bourgeois level, the accent necessarily shifts to emotional events. Since the script is shaped according to its original intention, with an eye on motion, the external plot recedes. Its emotional events are simple and lack content – indeed, they must lack content, for the sake of depth. Thus its psychological execution fails, due to the inarguable inadequacy of the manuscript. An expressionist poet and a psychological director, no matter how stylish, will not be able to get on together without compromise.

This compromise is the essential thing. For world view and stylistic purpose, when present in the film script, are closely related to expressionistic means of expression. Characteristic of this are several scripts by Henryk Galeen, an excellent psychological film novelist. He worked on the first Golem film and wrote *Nosferatu* and *Waxworks*. Galeen organizes his world around a very clear sense of style; he creates an intellectual living space in which the figures play by their own rules, yet are based on "understanding" and "empathy". But there's often a surprising bent in his scripts which only becomes clear through the construction of the gesture, the rhythmic realignment of the pictorial space, and the inclusion of unnatural forms. And that is why his name must be included here.

ACTORS

In the expressionist film, the actor is faced with a considerable challenge. He is meant to destroy the medium that ensures his camaraderie with the audience: rather than an artistic treatment of everyday language, rather than a heightened expression of the typical experience, he offers them a construct in which speech, tone and gesture are elements of his creative Will.

It must be noted at the outset that expressionist acting has developed into a comfortable place for dilettantes. A kind of decorative strongman has been nurtured, with what Alfred Kerr disdainfully terms "expressionistic concentration". Kerr lethally, and with potent toxins, undermines the externally conceived worldview of stage Expressionism. However, it seems to me that this great writer (we cannot call him otherwise, in fond tribute to all that we have learned from him) rejects the intellectual approach of Expressionism too strongly, out of human skepticism.

The actor who has discovered a suitable means of expression in the figurative world of Expressionism must develop his method with an eye toward a completely new ideal. Of course there is no such thing as a natural performance; of course the actor reshapes the natural object meaningfully and expediently in his domain. But it is one thing to elevate experienceable life to an intellectual level via stylish organization, and another to express this experienceable reality based on constructive Will, regardless of its normal counterpart. What this requires is a sacrifice of the effective conventional forms of expression, self-control, and an approach that defies psychological explanation.

Werner Krauss appears in *Caligari* to intuitively possess method and form. He is the actor who masters the incongruence between the conscience's processes and the body's posture in an expressionistic appearance, seemingly without effort. His mimicry has adjusted to the intellectual habitus. An intellectual element materializes, impetuous, sudden, and surprising, constructing the need for expression creatively, so to speak, rather than being coerced into it through emotions. Krauss' *Caligari* is virtually *the* exemplification of expressionistic acting, inasmuch as it does not attempt to overstep the boundaries of the theatrically

Figure 70. Ludwig Meidner, sketches for *The Street*.

operative. His outward performance seeks the direct, rigid forms of the architecture, is posed to express restraint, impenetrability and austere mutability. The moment it begins, the performance extracts every last bit of intensity – employing mimicry that replicates the oblique dips, sudden stops, and rolling curves of its environment. It is a performance of inventive abundance and not of natural limitation, for the psychological inventory of the actor is so evident that indeed, this form of expression represents an attempt to solve a timeless problem using new means.

The fact that these methods are part of a new consciousness is most evident in the last part of *Waxworks*, which Krauss dominates as Jack the Ripper. One cannot speak here of there being a series of events. A deliberately constructed figure is set in motion; the movements spill over into the dynamic values of the set and come to a head in Krauss's calculatedly impassive facial expression. It is a presence which seems emphatically timeless, due to the anxiety of the other two actors.

Expressionism is not the same as style in general: this fact must be kept

Colour Plate V. Alexandra Exner, costume sketches for *Salomé / The Three Sadducees.*

in mind especially when we evaluate films. The more consciously style-consciousness becomes a creative tool for the actor, the more amenable he is to expressionist forms. An actor of Emil Jannings' extraordinary format does not merely represent the ultimate in psychological dramatic art: as a psychological character study, his *Last Laugh* would have got mired in static monotony. But he achieved a profound effect because the

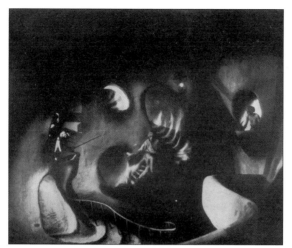

Figure 71. [Paul Leni,] *Waxworks* (Leni-Film Ufa).

character's predisposition is metaphysical, beyond the realm of daily experience, headed toward a meeting with Destiny. Certainly the psychological details of the performance are compelling, but the old man's scene of intoxication goes beyond that. It is the construction of a new form of existence, whose expressionistic manifestation is hindered only by the actor's unerring instinct for staying in touch with the audience. When he portrays Harun al-Rashid in *Waxworks,* the ambiguity of his performance nearly results in crisis. The director's intention swings between styles: one time, psychological drollery is meant to appeal; another time, the apparition is the powerful motor behind the creation. And thus the actor is not at home on any plane, on earth or in heaven.

Conrad Veidt is formed almost specifically by the expressionist film. An actor of unusual adaptability, he grew instantaneously into the fundamental problem with expressionist acting. His "Cesare" in *Caligari* is decisively attuned to the style of the film. His expression is sparing and inward; its accents are distributed with such conscious artistry, his character figures into the plot with so much compositional insight, that it can only be explained as arising from a kindred undercurrent of feeling about life. Veidt benefits from his external appearance, whose strict intellectuality is always engulfed by magical remoteness – though it is precisely the allure of his appearance that has often led him astray, when firm direction was not at hand. If however, the task and the creative Will are there to back him up, as in *Caligari*, the clarity of the vision is astonishing. A sensation that might typically be expressed through sobbing and breakdown is simplified to staring eyes, an uncertain gesture of the hand, a stretch of the body. It is simply the realization of a clearly identified, consciously organized concept.

This remove from daily life is what distinguishes the expressionist actor. Naturally questions of dramatic tact always come into play, since the actor on stage, as on film, is not a formal geometric element, but brings with him presuppositions to the audience's understanding. Ernst Deutsch, in *From Morn to Midnight*, tries to take a definitive leap out of his natural dimension. His cashier wears a suit and makeup and is painted with light – not as an expressionist uniform, but as a visible expression of the life of his conscience. Every gesture, every expression is grounded in this attitude: nowhere does the genuine behaviour of a suffering man influence his creation. The only crucial thing is that each nuance appears compositionally in its corresponding place in the world around him. He is subordinated to the stylistic purpose to such an extent that often, an inevitable automaton seems to be at work, rather than a living figure. If only the primal talent of this important actor were to suddenly break through, unexpectedly exploding the frame with a motion or a glance.

Expressionism reaches a crisis when its formal elements enlist living material that preserves its conventional meaning. For where life touches on life, wellsprings bubble up in an outbreak of nature. That is the one side of it. The other side is that the actor is not capable of prying himself away from the audience in the theatre seats. An emotional contact involuntarily takes hold which determines the shape and mode of expression on its own. This is not true to its principles, nor is it in the strict sense of the stage. But fire has no limits aside from God.

SET DESIGNERS

Expressionist form infiltrated film from the decorative element. The set is capable of setting up intellectual preconditions for the events that take place on it. Its style determines the mental attitude of the film.

As mentioned previously, the development of the *Caligari* film can be traced to the inspiration of the architects Warm, Röhricht and Reimann. If we look at their designs, our first impression is of how effortlessly the rigid expressionist forms are tailored to the psychological needs of the film. The decorative element, eliminated in pure works of art, takes on the function of communicating with the audience.

All the trusted forms of Expressionism come into play. The verticals stretch out diagonally, houses confine themselves at tilted angles, and surfaces become rhomboids. Simple kinetic tendencies of normal architecture, as expressed through verticals and horizontals, are transformed into a chaos of broken forms; motion has taken on a life of its own. These crooked roofs, these inclined surfaces, and these tilted walls staring into the air, all represent a release of energy. A movement begins, leaves its natural course, is caught up by another and directed elsewhere, curves again, and breaks. Meanwhile, as brightness and darkness are unleashed, the magical light performs, constructing, dividing, emphasizing, and destroying.

"The film set must become graphic art." The division of the spatial design through light, lines, and spaces laden with emotion, is the objective of the *Caligari* set. Consequently, the ornament takes on a supporting function: it structures the spaces, and its mysterious figures pull the soul along the wrong paths.

The cinematographer takes on a sizeable role. Hameister, who filmed *Caligari*, adapts himself to the architecturally-determined function of the light. And Carl Freund, Germany's most prominent cameraman, treats light as the decisive tool for space creation. Though he has not yet filmed a distinctly expressionist film, we sense to what extent the compositional power of light has embraced all his films.

Walter Reimann has clearly formulated the essential elements of expressionist set design. He bases landscape and street, wall and timberwork, on his passionately serious perception of the intellectual space of the film. His phantom on the rooftops of *Caligari* arises from the blueprint for the whole film, as do his figurines. If one compares them with Ludwig Meidner's designs for Grune's *The Street*, one immediately senses his adherence to principle. Meidner translates the wild dynamics of a nighttime cosmopolitan street into a vision of light, in which painterly techniques scatter the accents. His figure sketches for this film are autonomous individuals who, though indeed sustained by the spirit of the whole, also assert their life outside the image. The scenic realization of Grune's significant *Street* film adheres to the same creative technique, while the directors of Expressionism turn away from the experience of the world and toward new creation, based on a self-willed floor plan.

As Martin to Wiene, so Neppach behaves in relation to these designers. He takes reduction to the expressionist idiom seriously. He skirts psychological communication. The space is divided according to strict principles; light and dark are weighed according to a sense of rhythm; the character of the composition is preserved at all costs. His design is the framework for and definition of a plot that carries out the compositional thought with kinetic elements of form, so to speak. There is no need to approach the audience. Techniques are drawn exclusively from the artistic consciousness. Its whites and its darks are unreal: no light ever existed as this harsh blob; there never was a counterpart to these curvatures. The chairs, doors, and tables of the petit bourgeois room are forms in motion, swinging to the same rhythm as the process built into them: white lines, now strong, now weak, strongly accentuate their mobile nature. The bank entrance unleashes straining energies, animated by the idea of capital. The stairs are pulled apart into restless bodies of light that jump across to the figures and pass along their motion. The crowd at the six-day race is torn apart by lines of light – white flecks and lines, which lend wings to faces and clothing. The dynamics of this stadium, consumed as it is by motion, obsess the public and make them its supporters. They become purely expressive elements of its hard and noisy music.

Neppach's sets for *From Morn to Midnight* are ineffective. The same elements that pervade the production's pictorial space contribute to its crisis. As long as the designer's creation is based strictly on his Will, as long as he organizes the space based on his conception, he rips open a divide between himself and the viewers, which makes him unsuccessful. Partial possibilities ensue when he uses expressionist forms purely as a means of articulation, arranging them into the style of a set as transitions, supports, or decorative emphases. Though these admittedly do not establish a film as expressionist, they are useful in enhancing its expressive inventory.

Figure 72. Hans Poelzig, Golem city for *The Golem*.

6

LIMITATIONS OF THE EXPRESSIONIST FILM

The difficulty that expressionist film has in establishing itself lies not with a mutable outer constellation, but with its preconditions. For there can be no doubt that, with the exception of the surprise success of *Caligari,* the expressionist film has not found favour with the public.

To arrive at a categorical assessment, we must turn to the primary function that the cinema is accorded in the greater sphere of human industry. Film has a specific significance in the inventory of satisfying human needs. This has been proven clearly by the global success of film in the thirty years of its existence. If film were only a particularly folksy, cheaper form of the stage, it would long ago have killed off the theatre, having achieved no greater range than the stage reaches at best. Cursory statistical information already indicates that the effect of film on society is totally different, a mass phenomenon with individual colourations.

The success of the cinema can be explained by means of its engagement with an intrinsic biological human need. The daily depletion of people's energy, during which their cells are systematically degenerated, requires these cells to be rebuilt during breaks from work in the evening, which is achieved during sleep. This regenerative process requires a condition of intellectual relaxation, which is generally accompanied by a feeling of emptiness. This is where film comes in. It establishes new conditions for physiological rejuvenation; it leaves the viewer with his passive mood and still gives him the feeling of being intellectually occupied. This arousal can be absorbed so effortlessly that no or very little active intellectual effort is necessary. The cinema brings about the necessary feelings of relaxation that switch off consciousness of emptiness or boredom, without bringing with it an appreciable loss of balance.

The effortless apperception of film is thus one of its basic prerequisites. The viewer must be able to smoothly integrate the contents of the film into his world view, without this process requiring any form of intellectual activity. Expressionist film positions itself in basic opposition to this requirement, since its objective is the new structuring of formal elements based on a metaphysical intent. Psychology, the human soul's usual mode of transportation, is put out of service, so to speak, since expressionist film primarily involves comprehension rather than perception. Not empathy, but consideration.

The expressionist film tended to make concessions from the start. It looked for bridges to connect the separate worlds of the film and the audience, finally resigning itself to making expressionist means psychologically empathetic. *The Cabinet of Dr. Caligari* produces a richness of factors that provide mood, going even further by setting up a common platform between art and the viewer: the plot involves the hallucination of a lunatic who, following his natural inclination, experiences the world as a distortion and a grimace. This is already an admission that the expressionist film, in its pure state, must remain opaque to the viewer. Its artistic form requires a commentary afterward, an excuse. This tendency continues in all films of this kind, which live off dreams and occult powers. Expressionist film is not capable of surviving as a pure art, and the first to recognize this fact were its inventers themselves.

The linchpin of this crisis of understanding is the human being on film. The artist can create the active being in film to whatever extent required; he can completely alter his natural form, or construct it anew, from the ground up. The fact remains that the viewer in the theatre identifies with "the person". No matter how man expresses himself on film, the moment he no longer expresses the soul of the viewer, contact breaks off, and understanding and interest cease. The viewer tends to admit that, in

Figure 73. Tristan Tzara, programme.

principle, bold exaltations of the spirit might be possible. In order for him to conceive of the film's plot as "real" though, it must simply be possible for him to imagine that a person could act that way. If this congruence cannot be brought about, the film remains an inassimilable foreign body and is meaningless to the audience.

This presents an opportunity for the absolute film, which categorically eliminates the possibility of comparing formal elements – the film's "supporting players" – with the audience. The natural object is neutralized and stripped of all accompanying sentiments. Line and surface speak as spatial components: if a natural object appears, it is an element in space, and has no intellectual value. A plate is not a utensil from which to eat but a concave disc, which behaves in varying ways in space. There

135

is no value placed on it. It is clear that extraordinary activity on the part of the viewer is required in order for the process to be translated into a sphere of "understanding", though only elemental energies are visualized. This brings with it many implications.

Easy perception, and an effortless sorting into the viewer's conceptual world, are not just strict prerequisites for film as it attempts to realize its biological function. They are required in order for film to be a commodity – which is the only way it can be distributed in a manner in keeping with its physiological task. That is why film is an industry, and has no life outside of industry.

When one views film as a commodity, Expressionism becomes nearly irrelevant. This consideration is purely mathematical. Taken schematically, a manufactured good may not cost more to make than it normally yields when the prevailing profit margin is added to it. It must be at least feasible to achieve the required volume of sales. A low estimate of the number of film consumers in Germany is around ten million people, with a correspondingly larger number abroad. Any film that does not appeal to the masses is harmful to the German film industry since it narrows its capital base. Film is making its way in Germany from the metropolis to the smallest village. As differentiated as the human intellect is, by virtue of people's profession and education, there nonetheless exists among them a certain emotional homogeneity, which of itself bodes well for film's survival. The differences do not exist as far as commerce is concerned: only that which conforms to universal constants enables profitability – and thereby the continued existence of the film industry.

Insofar as the expressionist film incorporates these conditions, it still has prospects, from a purely commercial point of view. The more it retains its fundamental principles though, and the more rigorously it aspires to present a unique creation of reality, the more it loses itself in commercial insubstantiality. It only remains to point out that an expressionist film's qualities might be used to pollinate, to open up new avenues of expression for the film industry as a whole. But obviously the exceptional nature of such a phenomenon would be part of the debate itself. A case like this will be exceedingly rare.

7

PERSPECTIVES

The German film has developed along a straight line. First with a definite eye on quantity, then toward a nearly complete inventory of creative techniques. There has undeniably been a recent, visible tendency toward the qualitative exploitation of resources, a proclivity that reaches from big pictures to chamber dramas. The influence of American film has played a substantial role in this development.

The German film is invested in dramatic content, strong characters and passionate events: the American film tends more toward entertainment, agreeably polished figures, and harmless thrills. The German manuscript comes to a head over catastrophes; its figures perpetually assume an intellectual fencing stance. In America, the plot flows uninterruptedly, the characters develop pointedly, and the nuance, rather than the emotion-laden event, is operative. Seen at a distance, American films appear more polished, more uniform; there's a certain family resemblance among them. This explains the audience's unquestioning acceptance of them, whereas the word "analytical" has been mobilized abroad against the German film.

The contact of the two continents has had visible effects. The American film recognizes that the audience's familiarity with its unvarying appearance diminishes its thrill factor. The German film attempts to extricate itself from its prestissimo of events, and to bring character and plot into a harmonious relationship. This new accent on the character and refinement of expressive technique requires an enrichment of creative forms. Whereas in America, the lighting is a means to obtaining steady, wonderfully clear set illumination, the German prefers effects, treating light as a factor that creates space and confers greater freedom on the camera. In general, he still means to elucidate a general feeling about the world, to film the "spirit" of the plot. Here Expressionism effectively becomes a vehicle of communication.

Though Expressionism as a closed art form will be rejected, its individual forms of expression will continue to be eagerly utilized. There are moods of a landscape that cannot be photographed by normal means. The "spirit" of an illuminated city street is incomprehensible to the camera lens, unless the image to be recorded is deliberately created by a constructive Will. Expressionism will be used whenever effects are called for that cannot be tangibly reproduced using a natural object, but can only be experienced intellectually. And this is true in general, for all means of expression that are effective in film.

Expressionism as a strict art form is no longer current. New independent solutions are coming into play, whereby the broad use of the term "Expressionism" might keep the name alive for a long time after the intellectual attitude has completely changed.

It may be seen as an advantage that the German film industry was the first to come up with the tools for expressionist film, thus demonstrating the necessity of enhancing the expressive world of film with new forms. Whether or not it meets with commercial success is of less importance than its general task, which is to keep the course of history flowing. Wherever there is movement, there is change in the world; uniformity is paralysis of the soul. All paths lead toward the goal, but only a bolt of lightning can spark a flame.

Afterword

Christian Kiening and Ulrich Johannes Beil

I

The relationship between Expressionism and film is suggestive yet indistinct. Ill-disposed to a naturalistic depiction of reality, Expressionism came to film late, after it had already reached painting, literature, music and theater. But soon it seemed as though Expressionism had only really come into its own with film – as though, by fusing the radically subjective expressive art with the dynamic medium that combines closeness and distance, it discovered something that could enrich each of them in turn. Even for many contemporaries, expressionist elements were considered the signature of the art film: "film perfectly embodied this new life expression, creating a common yet fragmented rhythm between things and people".[1] In particular, film historians after the Second World War left the impression that German film between 1918 and 1933 could be correlated with Expressionism in general, or that expressionist film could be understood as the embodiment of Weimar cinema. Lotte H. Eisner made a considerable contribution to this impression in her *Haunted Screen*, which first appeared in 1952 in Paris.[2] Just a few indicators were enough for her to label a film "expressionist"; other stylistic elements were marginalized, or remained unmentioned. And even after Eisner herself qualified her far-reaching concept of Expressionism,[3] a more precise description of "expressionist film" was long inhibited. Even fifty years later, Sabine Hake noted that

139

the term raised more questions than it answered.[4] Does it refer to a style, a movement, a period, or an epistemology? Does it concern narrative motifs or imaginary constellations? Does it denominate an artistic rebellion or the manifestation of contradictions within Weimar society? Since the answer to the question of which films could be categorized as "expressionist" depends on the extension of the word "Expressionism", one could not even say for sure whether Expressionism was a German contribution to the European film avant-garde, or a cinematic "special path" that differentiated German from international cinema.[5]

There is probably no better way to approach questions like these than by returning to the book that represents the early milestone of historical discourse on expressionist film: *Expressionism and Film,* published in 1926 in Berlin's *Lichtbildbühne* publishing house. Its author, Rudolf Kurtz (born in Berlin December 31, 1884; died there on July 26, 1960), was doubly predestined for the subject – he was deeply affiliated with Expressionism, and he had an intimate knowledge of the film scene. Kurtz began to write at age 19, encouraged by Alfred Kerr; he studied German, Philosophy and National Economy, founded the *Schall und Rauch* ("Sound and Smoke") cabaret in 1909, and between 1910 and 1914, accompanied the formation of the expressionist "movement" with a multitude of essays, lampoons, reviews, and commentaries.[6]

Kurt Tucholsky already notes of the 28-year-old in 1912 that he "happens to be one of the finest writers", and besides, he knows "practically everybody who ever went to the old *Café des Westens*".[7] Rudolf Leonhard praises Kurtz's foreword to Marinetti's *Manifesto of Futurism*, which Kurtz had introduced to Berlin, for its "successful, cautiously ambiguous and concise compactness".[8] Else Lasker-Schüler calls him one of the "venerable Berlin pashas" and admires his "intimate writing style".[9] Fritz Max Cahén tells of a "fierce debate over the significance of categories" in Kurtz's apartment outside the city gates.[10] Ernst Blass recalls "Rudolf Kurtz's fine sensitivity and astute capacity for classification", and describes the intellectually stimulating, unconventional, and congenial atmosphere in the soon-to-be legendary *Café des Westens*: "Van Gogh was in the air, as were Nietzsche, Freud, and Wedekind. We were searching for a post-rational Dionysus. Van Gogh represented expression and experience, opposition to Impressionism and Naturalism; blazing concentration, youthful authenticity, immediacy, depth of subject, exhibition and hallucination. Someone else came up with the word 'Expressionism'; but in our circles, we had long sailed on expressionist waters ... We spoke of 'visions'."[11] In the *Café des Westens*, publishers and authors rubbed elbows; there were revolutionaries and dreamers, artists and actors – and probably an increasing number of filmmakers, following the publication of Pinthus's *Kinobuch* ("Cinema Book", 1913), whose authors had opened themselves to all things cinematic. Kurtz himself provided an overview of these characters in his contribution to Mack's book *Die Zappelnde Leinwand* ("The Fidgety Screen", 1916).[12]

Despite all his interest in art criticism and film aesthetics, Kurtz was no sensitive aesthete. A man of versatile interests, intellectually disposed, and a presence on the publishing scene, he consistently voiced strong opinions about the cultural wars of the time.[13] His gift of observation, his esprit, and his familiarity with the avant-garde movements commanded the respect of his contemporaries. At the same time, he stood in the shadow of his colleagues at *Der Sturm* and *Aktion*, the student "neo-pathetics" who founded their club and cabaret in 1909 in Berlin's *Hackeschen Höfe*, inspired by Jakob van Hoddis's poem *Weltende* ("World's End"). While the names of Kurt Hiller, Herwarth Walden, Franz Pfemfert, Ferdinand Hardekopf, Carl Einstein and Erich Mühsam long remained tied to the modern literary spirit, Kurtz "left the poor men of letters"[14] early on. Having little in common with the subcultural expressionists and eccentric authors, he sought employment in institutions, film production, the press, and the media. After 1916, he acted as a dramaturge and, for almost a decade, held leading positions at Projekts AG "Union", which later absorbed into Universum Film AG (Ufa). At the time of the writing of *Expressionism and Film*, he was chief editor at the *Lichtbildbühne*, the first and, for many years, most important weekly magazine on the German film scene, which had been started by Karl Wolffsohn in 1908. The position Kurtz took in a 1921 argument with Hans Siemsen and Kurt Tucholsky, regarding the extent to which a film's success is dependent on the size of the production, shows him firmly on the side of the industry: "Without money, without lots of money, all these wonderful things are useless, because you're stuck with a cheap set and bad material. The Siemsens are unaware of this; they just sit at their desks and haven't the slightest clue." If your production has millions to spend, he says, it means "you have decent technical support; it means you attract the best possible actors; it means you team up with artistic workers; it means you travel to scenic locations".[15]

Kurtz was concerned with the effect of film (even the artificial variety) as a mass medium, and his popular comedic plays, adventure books, and cheery novels of the 30s targeted a mass market. Mostly published by the Berlin *Drei Masken* or *Arcadia* publishing houses, and partly concerned with film or radio, they served as meal tickets at a time when there was no market for literary or artistic avant-gardism.[16] These works, which capitalized on his knowledge of various media, were accompanied by confident contributions in the areas where literature and film intersect – there was for instance a series on the "History of the Film Manuscript" (1934) and a biography of the actor Emil Jannings (1942).[17] As the successful founder, publisher and chief editor of *Nacht-Express* ("Night Express"), a lively, left-leaning tabloid which ran from late 1945 through 1953 in Berlin's Soviet sector, Kurtz proved he had a nose for contemporary publishing trends.[18] However, he was unable to complete the autobiography that he worked on in his later years, and he did not live long enough to see *Expressionism and Film* rediscovered. On the occasion of the international film book exhibit in Venice in 1965, the book was awarded the main prize in Category VIII. Reprinted in the same year, it introduced a series of film studies texts. In the 1980s, it was translated into Italian and French (but published without the illustrations). Even now, it turns up in nearly every silent film programme and on every silent film website whose authors aim for a clear and concise description of expressionist film.[19]

II

This book is a work on the threshold. It was published in 1926, the year Hans Ulrich Gumbrecht presented as being unremarkably "at the edge of time".[20] That year, there was a dangerous increase in the publication of patriotic novels and militant war books in popular literature (which Hans Sahl, analyzing them in the magazine *Tagebuch*, called "the rise of dark, sinister powers that boded ill, waiting for their moment in history"[21]). Also that year, there were media upheavals tied to the introduction of radio. On October 23, 1923, the first official one-hour programme "on station 400" had been broadcast from the top floor of the VOX building in Berlin; the *Reichs-Rundfunk-Gesellschaft* or RRG (Reich Radio Society) was founded on May 15, 1925. This led people to ponder the effects of the new medium, to look "thought transfer by radio" in the eye, and to imagine a "radio police" or "radio man".[22] If people had only just identified the power of film "with its endless manoeuvrability" and "the complete freedom with which this apparatus masters space and time",[23] now radio promised a means of communication that was even more capable of transcending space, and more limitless, and which gave "everyone the opportunity to live in, and experience, the community of people who share the same language and like minds".[24] Indeed, people began thinking in a more basic way about the relationship between objects and media,[25] the electrophysiological conditions of broadcasting (also between humans and machines),[26] and the role of the masses in the face of the new media.[27]

Not only had more and more people become increasingly versatile 'media consumers'; the media themselves liaised between entities of increasingly greater magnitude. The film industry had taken on such proportions by 1926 that it could be seen as the dubious machinery of beautiful but false illusions. For instance, Siegfried Kracauer describes the Ufa film studio in Neubabelsberg near Potsdam as an alternate world, pieced together of movable sets: "the entire macrocosm seems to be gathered in this new version of Noah's ark. But the things that rendezvous here do not belong to reality. They are copies and distortions that have been ripped out of time and jumbled together. They stand motionless, full of meaning from the front, while from the rear they are just empty nothingness. A bad dream about objects that has been forced into the corporeal realm [...]. On the meadows and hills the inventory organizes itself into patterns. Architectural constructions jut upward as if meant to be inhabited. But they represent only the external aspects of the prototypes, much the way language maintains facades of words whose original meaning has vanished."[28] Such contemporary gigantism led to retrospection, especially regarding film's rapid development. In April 1926, the illustrator, author and director Edmund Edel noted in his *Unvollkommene Erinnerungen* ("Unfinished Memories") of the period following 1912: "The cinema, and film, suddenly leapt into the conversation; you could no longer simply write off the movement. People of intellect, and people who rejected the intellect of others, discovered film's exalted mission. They surged into the elegant cinemas, to relieve themselves from the daily hustle and bustle for a few hours, to be transported to the faraway places of their dreams, to thrill to the sensations of criminal, social or emotional conflicts, or to refresh their nerves by laughing themselves silly over grotesque buffoonery. It was a short path from suburban cinemas to splendorous palaces: in barely two decades, Berlin became the movie theatre capital of the world."[29]

Kurtz lived through these decades, and he registered the change that had been ongoing since about 1920. *Expressionism and Film* is aware of its position on the threshold of the development of avant-garde art and the medium of film. Kurtz recognizes that a discourse is forming in which Expressionism and film are becoming entangled in various ways. But he is also aware of his distance from this discourse, which had been abandoned by 1926 and was only just then allowing for reflection. He manages to combine analytical astuteness with emotional identification. He is able to accurately characterize and evaluate films, describing them 'from inside out' due to his intimate knowledge of the experimental laboratories of the time. He makes them feel current again as they pass before our inner eye, on the strength of language that is steeped in the energy of its topic. But he also sketches a chronology, works out paradigms, and creates a small canon. He illustrates the tendencies, art forms, and discourses to which the films correspond. He conceptualizes a future perspective, and he pursues the question of whether, and how, the legacy of the expressionist 'movement' still plays a role in the context of such competing styles.

If the change as outlined here deals primarily with the film *production* of the time, it also concerns film *theory* which at these years began to look at film as a medial and cultural "Gesamtkunstwerk". In 1924, Béla Balázs's *Visible Man, or the Culture of Film* is published, celebrating film as a rediscovery of the sensory and visual in an age of intellectualization and abstraction.[30] Rudolf Harms's 1926 *Philosophy of Film* sees man against a "black-and-white surface, endowed with motion" as melded with the cosmos, the logos, the "very beginning and very end" of life.[31] A reviewer of Kurtz's book notes that the medium itself was not as interesting as the change in perceived reality that went along with it: "It is not film which is diagnosed at all, but rather a philosophy that is about to emerge in, and from, a new art form – wherein film too will discover *its true nature*".[32]

Affinities between Expressionism and film were perceived early on. The German 'auteur film' was inaugurated in 1912, starting with a contract between the largest German film corporation and the playwrights' union.[33] From then on, it was socially acceptable to speak of an aesthetic of the cinema, and to mention the medium (initially derided by the feuilletons as trivial) in the same breath as literature and theatre. In his 1913 "Gedanken zu einer Ästhetik des Kinos" ("Thoughts on an Aesthetic of the Cinema"), published a few weeks following the premiere of THE STUDENT OF PRAGUE, György Lukács singles out the fantastic elements, the movement, the everything-is-possible quality of the cinema, as well as its affinity to the "fairy-tale" and "dream". He puts forth that its "liveliness" and "truth to nature" were due to the cinema's turning away from the static human- and word-based art of the stage from the very start, which seems to philosopher Lukács to be *Greek in its very essence*". Lukács determines prophetically that the technical capabilities of film (reverse, fast motion, cuts) were creating a "world like that of E. T. A. Hoffmann or Poe [...], Arnim or Barbey d'Aurevilly"; he already claims that film has expressionist potential. The only thing missing is the new "great poet" of the cinema, to "interpret and order this world, and to transform its merely technical, haphazard fantasy into something metaphysically meaningful, into pure style [...]".[34] That same year, while pondering the "capabilities of cinema art", Paul Ernst also grapples with dimensions of the "grotesque and fantastic". While he certainly considers them to have potential, he feels the film's intrusively mechanical, intellectually remote aspects still keep it from being taken seriously as a "work of art".[35]

The ties between Expressionism and film are taken more for granted during the First World War. Kurt Pinthus fires the collective starting shot in 1914 with his previously-mentioned *Kinobuch*, a collection of cinematic prose sketches stemming from the pens of authors close to Expressionism, such as Max Brod, Alfred Ehrenstein, and Else Lasker-Schüler. In the foreword he differentiates between cinema and theatre, drawing attention to specifically cinematic terms such as 'milieu', 'action' and 'trick'. He mentions expressionist keywords rather incidentally, touching instead on key aspects of the contemporary film industry, such as its ambitions toward world domination and its imaginative use of design. The audience wants "not just to see something realistic, but rather to see a realistic thing elevated to a more ideal, fantastic sphere". The "cinema piece" attempts to "stir up the craving that all people suppress, namely to experience and embrace all human destinies, and all that happens throughout the world. And then it seeks to satisfy that craving …".[36] Bernhard Diebold goes even further in a series of articles on "Expressionism and Cinema" in the *Neue Zürcher Zeitung* of September 1916. Tracing the Heraclitean, dynamic tendencies of expressionist painting and music, he enthuses about the basic cinematic element of "motion" and its release of "kinetic energies". As the "realization of Expressionism" he imagines an art form which still doesn't recognize itself as such. The "cinema", or more precisely "film drawn by an artist", is a painting set to motion and musical rhythm, which will rise "freely" above every "human shape, and nature-bound appearance of any kind".[37]

Following the First World War, Expressionism has reached a level of general popularity. Whereas it has previously been relegated to rather elitist circles and small stages, as well as newspapers and catalogues with low circulations, its connection to film is now well-established. Carl Hauptmann sees the possibility of regaining "the *primal meaning*, the *gestural meaning*" of words precisely through film's lack of dialogue. He finds the immediate presence of things set in motion to be particularly expressionist: "*All* expressionist artists have been striving for years to achieve just such an innovative, vibrant, immediate, abrupt *primal communication of the soul*". Thus the "bioscope" cinema is "one of the most significant discoveries in the arts", and holds out the prospect of a "rich future".[38] Gertrud David calls explicitly for filmmakers to make use of expressionist methods so that they may create their own style.[39] Carlo Mierendorff ties the new cinematic technology to avant-garde art, celebrating the relationship between cinematic representation and reception as a comprehensive expressionist phenomenon: "Who can still escape? Whiteness flashes. Blackness scurries. Light scatters. Vibration is sweet stupefaction. The rush lulls us to sleep. Steam rises from the skin! Swirling vapor impregnates the senses. [...] Embraced. Whispered. Applause. Hello. Protest. Bug-eyes. Smut. Smirks. [...] From machine halls and warehouses, from cellars and tenements, from country houses and Eastern suburbs, from subways, trams, foundries, factories and offices, Man rises up. In endless procession, to the cinemas of the great cities and provincial towns."[40] Here the sociological context of the cinema itself receives an expressionist interpretation. The essayist's language is infected by his topic: a single expressionist stream of social energy flows from the subject of film to its production, screening, and acceptance across social classes, and all the way through to his reflection. Kurtz will adopt this method in *Expressionism and Film*.

With the expressionists' interest in film, the front lines between the artistic avant-garde and down-to-earth mass entertainment, between the cultural elite and capitalistically-driven promotional interests, began to blur. Representatives of a subculture were now addressing a mass audience via the movie screen. Poets, novelists and dramatists, painters, graphic artists and set designers sensed the cinema's new effectiveness as a mass medium, and saw it as a challenge. In film, they met 'moguls' who hoped to profile new products and tap new markets by admitting artistic elements into their films.[41] Any last barriers between Expressionism and film fell following the sensational premiere of THE CABINET OF DR. CALIGARI on February 26, 1920, in Berlin's Marmorhaus Theater. Even during its filming, J. Brandt praised in the *Film-Kurier* Robert Wiene's direction for mediating auspiciously between drama and painting; he found the film capable of holding its "own line". Following a visit to the studio, he raved about the "pioneering work" which had enabled the "Expressionism" to finally "make its way into film art".[42] In other reviews as well, CALIGARI is celebrated as the "first expressionist film",[43] and as "a new page in the history of film".[44] One writer enthused about a "nerve-wrackingly bizarre frenzy of images", which needn't shy away from comparisons with "Poe, Hoffmann, or Meyrink".[45] For the first time, film was seen as "elevated from the realm of photography to the pure sphere of the artwork".[46] One noted a "radical change", "like the one we saw in theatrical performances, when actors crossed from the realistic set to the proscenium arch.[47] The *Münchner Neueste Nachrichten* goes so far as to claim that "film itself" is "expressionist", and that a true "modern 'art film theory' would develop out of expressionist scenography".[48] CALIGARI director Wiene himself draws attention to the substantial association between Expressionism and film in the *Berliner Börsen-Courier*, claiming that when a film was meant to achieve a certain quality standard and "engage artistic workers", he would reach out "inevitably to Expressionism".[49] These artistic workers consisted of the writers, illustrators and outfitters who designed the scenarios that were set to film. Often they were haunting, oppressive scenarios: in 1921 the Dutch painter Frits van den Berghe combined Impressionism and Expressionism in his image entitled *Cinema*, which dramatizes Expressionism's closeness to film and freakishness. A naked woman flees through a movie theatre toward the light of the projector, pursued by two giant, threatening, bull-like men. The horror that it calls forth crosses the line between the events on-screen and in front of it, reaching from two-dimensionality into three-dimensionality.[50]

The expressionist film à la CALIGARI becomes a paradigm of what art is capable of during the course of rapid modern medial change – including public education. Julius Sternheim maintains that people for whom "Expressionism" "was [previously] only an empty word [...] will see in these images [...] how Expressionism injects the desired mood into an on-screen situation [...]" – in other words, how Expressionism functions in the hands of a virtuosic mass medium.[51] Béla Balázs (and following

Frits van den Berghe, *Cinema* (1921).

him, Harms) takes an ontological approach, identifying the quintessential artistic effort that film makes to highlight the 'physiognomy of objects' through Expressionism. "No art is as well qualified to represent this 'face of things' as film. For film presents not just a once-and-for-all rigid physiognomy, but a mysterious play of expressions. It is quite certain that film is the true terrain, perhaps the only legitimate home, of expressionism. And this is indeed the style towards which all modern films are moving without wishing to do so, or even noticing that they are doing so."[52]

Notwithstanding the expressionist mood of the early 1920s that pervaded many areas, enthusiasm about its outlook for film was never unanimous. Some were put off by its supposedly elitist style; some worried about the productions' appeal to the public; some were afraid, even as they admired it, that it might catch on and revolutionize the entire filmmaking industry.[53] Aesthetic objections are directed toward inconsistency and disconnectedness – between plot and décor, for instance[54] – or the unnecessary violation of the "anatomy" of "nature".[55] When CALIGARI is reissued in 1925, Rudolf Arnheim, in a critical piece in *Stachelschwein* entitled "Dr. Caligari redivivus", scoffs at the décor, which by then decorates "the walls of even the humblest cafes", and mocks the "figures that move around in this gaudy fuss and bother". They are "not stylized in the least; they have regular actors' faces, wearable clothes, and natural gestures, and we hold it against these poor people that their behinds are constructed according to the laws of organic structure".[56]

Ultimately, behind these and similar objections lies a sense of the inner ambiguity of expressionist film: its adherence to object presence on the one hand, and its dismissal of naturalism on the other. Or: its fascination with both the reproductive and the creative aspects of film. Expressionist productions, despite their intent to stylize, work with living actors and their nuance-filled "physiognomy" (Balázs). The productions count on mimetic density – newly achievable in the medium of cinema – which simultaneously dissipates in the abstract, artificial décor and sets. Expressionist film works to get beyond the irresolvable interpenetration of contradictory factors by confronting the naturalistic, immediate elements of the film medium with a forced artificiality, a 'Kunstwollen'.[57] One could label this a scandal, an attack against the physical authenticity of film, but also as possibility to gain authenticity precisely through artificiality. In this view, the artificial generation of intensity, dynamics, and disturbances in everyday perception – plus the alienating effects that go with them – is surprisingly suited to create a new form of emotionally effective authenticity.

What we encounter here is one of Expressionism's general ambiguities, which, around 1920, became more and more visible. In 1918, in a longer unpublished essay, Siegfried Kracauer sees in Expressionism a "beginning" and a "stage" on the path toward "liberation of minds", but at the same time "a *call* for action and art, rather than real action and real art, and a suspicious amount of polishing up of the whole movement through talk about ideologies".[58] After 1920, the number of requiems for the once promising awakening begins to increase.[59] Oskar Loerke feels the "rush of recognition" departing.[60] Robert Müller speaks ironically of "Depressionism".[61] Wilhelm Worringer imagines a process of self-exhaustion: "Though Expressionism may still greedily spread out its aerial roots in all directions today, the space around it has been sucked dry and empty, yielding nothing more in the way of living nutrients".[62] In selling itself, Worringer claims, Expressionism had taken over various areas of society and thereby endangered its "essence"; even if this essence had been "mere fiction", it was nonetheless a fiction "filled with secret suffering". The omnipresent "*business* of art", "this menacing shell game whose shells are already half-empty", had set in motion a widespread aestheticization that resulted in the disappearance of the "spontaneous generation of instinct" and "the immediacy of sensual experience".[63] The bywords now are 'post-Expressionism', 'Magic Realism', and 'Surrealism'.[64] Important 1925 exhibits display *New Objectivity* in Mannheim, and *Art abstrait* in Paris. Each counters, in its own way, the disappearance of revelatory immediacy with an orientation toward the everyday, free from metaphysical ballast.

Kurtz's dissociation from the subject doesn't go this far. To him, delineating the limitations of expressionist film is not the same thing as writing a requiem for the era. Notwithstanding all the swan songs, he tries to recapture the electrifying aspects of Expressionism by portraying its vitality, its extension into a wide variety of fields and discourses, its reflections, dynamics and paradoxes, and its continuing effects under changing circumstances. He finds the organizational constructivism, and secular metaphysics, of a forceful, creative Will in politics as well as in Jensen's machine worlds and Picasso's pictures. He discerns in the expressionist film – as an interface between elite art and mass media – new, unimagined opportunities for interlacing authenticity with artificiality. And he attempts to map out these possibilities in his book, precisely at a point in time when film itself is about to take leave from expressionist artificiality, and to transform it. Similar to Balázs, who understands film's specific authenticity as being uniquely suited to Expressionism,[65] Kurtz takes expressionist film as an open form exceeding binary codes.

III

Kurtz does not set out to write a history of expressionist film. He is illuminating a relationship, a tension-ridden space from which he can gain a specific vantage point on his own time. In the foreword, he calls his work "aphoristic" and says it is its task "to allow its methodic disposition to prove useful to readers with as wide a range of experience as possible". The 'methodic disposition' would be the systematic relationship between the chapter titles. The 'wide range of experience' would be the interface between Expressionism and the film circles where Kurtz, as indicated, had moved for decades, between the Expressionist and Futurist groups on the one hand, and working film critics on the other. Many of the protagonists in *Expressionism and Film* were known to him personally; he was engaged in an animated exchange with Ernst Lubitsch, who had used an artificial, fantastically grotesque set in THE WILD CAT (1918).[66] He was a friend of Emil Jannings, who made an impression as Harun al Raschid in Paul Leni's WAXWORKS (1923). Kurtz was also a friend of Leni himself; he had written the script for his exotic adventure film THE MYSTERY OF BANGALORE (1917). *Expressionism and Film* is dedicated to Jannings, "the man, the artist, the friend";[67] Leni the painter, stage designer, graphic artist and film director was assigned the job of designing the sophisticated cover art. Also in Kurtz's circle of friends were Karlheinz Martin, the Berlin-based theatre director responsible for FROM MORN TO MIDNIGHT, THE HOUSE ON THE MOON (both 1920), and the avant-garde artists Viking Eggeling, Hans Richter and Francis Picabia. His succinct assessments come from intimate insight into their works. From his confident familiarity with the film and art scene emerges the nuanced language, and the equivocal reflection, which have made the book not only a classic point of reference for the history of expressionist film, but one of the most-cited early film books.

One thing that neither the older editions nor this one can make visible is that *Expressionism and Film* is an art book. Its large format (21.5 × 27 cm) and wide margins, 73 black and white illustrations in the text and 5 colour reproduction plates, made it one of the expensive bibliophilic highlights of the 1920s (original price: 16 Reichsmarks). As such it stands out in the catalogue of the *Lichtbildbühne* publishing house, which was an important institution for filmmakers of the period and had its eye on the industry as well. *Lichtbildbühne* had published the *Film Industry Yearbook* since 1922/23, and in 1926 it printed Egon Jacobsohn's and Kurt Mühsam's *Lexicon of Film*. Shortly thereafter, *Wie ich zum Film kam* (*How I Got Started in Film*, 4 Reichsmarks) launched the *Books on the Industry* series, with volumes like *The Practical Cameraman* (Seeber, 1927; 5 Reichsmarks) and *Film Direction and the Film Script* (Pudovkin, 1928; 5 Reichsmarks). *Expressionism and Film* operates in a different aesthetic dimension. Its images – paintings, sketches, stills – simultaneously illustrate and dynamize its subjects. Occasionally film strips run parallel to the text, lending it an expressionist style as the films are being described. Kurtz contributed to FROM MORN TO MIDNIGHT, with retrospect perhaps the most expressionist of all expressionist films, by an arrangement with its author Georg Kaiser. His description of the film runs thus: "A lightbulb goes off in the cashier's brain. To see the world, to live, to break out, to lust, to grab for once with both hands, everywhere, somewhere. He steals; he disappears, taking the money with him. Apoplexy in the family, hoarse astonishment at the bank. And the police reach out after him with grasping, spider-like arms … but the cashier is on a pilgrimage to the good life. Somewhere, there's a flash of recognition: life is not on the surface, life must come from within. Conversation with a fantastic skeleton on a scrubby tree in the winter night, which comes back to life, stretches its branches, and clasps languidly like an octopus. Life to the full, life in all its grandeur. Vices, whores, bright lights; the cashier in a tailcoat, noble, superior, crème. The behaviour of an exuberant spendthrift, throwing money around with both hands – but the gesture is an empty one; the money remains in his coat pocket. Women coo over him, heads bow down low, soft hands caress his cheeks – a throaty laugh; is this life? Dance around the strongbox. What was blossoming becomes ragged, woman turns to death's-head. And thus, whipped by his own shadow along the edge of the abyss, he hurtles toward the steadfast engine of charity: the Salvation Army. There she stands, a girl in uniform, a slender creature removed from life, pathetic, all rough penance, all sobbed prayers on the sinner's bench. Is this life? Confession? Repenting, kneeling with wrung hands? He follows her greedily, the only merciful one, and also the one who always mocked him, in many forms – the bleak death's head. And she has already whispered his name to the police, the police burst in, with a blast of trumpets and ring-around-the-rosy prayers – a stumbling, the skull, all is death, the carefully made-up mask of life. Life? Light reflected on steel: a pressure, a flash; the semi-automatic has closed the account. What is life? A hunt, from morn to midnight, for one's soul, for the true, immortal soul. A span of dreams, between greed and finale." (70sq.)

Whenever Kurtz describes a film's content and sequence, expressionist prose blazes the way, characterized by ellipses and oxymorons, staccato sounds and the pathos of existence. This indicates the literary context of the films, and the problem of representing them verbally: formally diverse and non-uniform, fantastic and erratic, their tendency to erase the boundaries of bodies, space, and line necessitates in turn a language without boundaries – or a word-image collage, like the one Leni designs for the cover. Kurtz will write in Leni's obituary a few years later: "He discovered for himself the life of light, the immense power of the play between lightness and heaviness, semi-darkness and shadow. Even before Expressionism constructed reality based on its own laws of creation, Leni unsettled souls tragically, by means of light, in a *Drama of the Unconscious* which took hold more deeply, and much more mystically, than the clearly-defined world of corporeality."[68] We see this too in Leni's collage: letters combine with images, lines with fragments of bodies, clips from films and magazines with painterly elements; all are bound together by an off-center center, a cubist spinning top from which the objects emerge to produce a hypnotic effect. The image is designed to entrance, to entice, to hold tight to the viewer. Its photographic elements – the endless row of half-naked bodies, the female eyes fixed on us – produce a tension between viewing and being viewed, which finds its counterpart in the expressionist play of surface and depth.

Like its cover, the book spans a wide range. It describes, evokes and analyzes; its themes include aesthetics and industry, avant-garde experiment and bourgeois ambiance, the attitude toward life, literature, art, music, and architecture – all of which meet up together in the medium

Paul Leni, *Expressionism and Film* (1926)

of film. Its point of departure is that Expressionism is a way of seeing the world rather than an artistic movement – and from the outset, this understanding corresponds to the modern tendency to express "inner-most man". In 1911, the year 'Expressionism' was first used in connec-tion with French Fauvist painting and the literature of the new generation, Kurtz formulated it thus: "The young generation. They express themselves; they act out, screaming forth their inner world in a storm of excitement, immersing themselves in a profusion of murky shapes, resplendent with triumphant indignation: this is the way new generations herald their arrival. They express themselves in the fire of enthusiasm, casting off the burden of a sluggish era in giddy revolution; express themselves, reclaiming the freedom of their spirits in the blazing current of events. This strikes me more as the passion of insightful people than do the artificial efforts coming out of Nouveau Weimar, where verses stick in the actors' throats."[69]

Starting around 1920, as new abstract and realistic artistic directions gained ground, this generation's desire for ideological greatness had already taken on a certain patina, as mentioned previously.[70] Yvan Goll summed it up: "All that Expressionism (1910–1920) wasn't the name of an artistic form, but of a *disposition*. Far more a philosophy than the result of a need to produce art".[71] In his famous anthology *Menschheitsdämmerung* [1919], Kurt Pinthus collected "literature which we call the 'newest', or 'expressionist', because it is all eruption, explosion, intensity". It is, he says, the prophetic expression of a historical, even anthropological, constellation: "The art of an epoch does not cause events […], but is rather an indicative symptom, the intellectual flowering from the same humus as the later real happening. It is itself an event in time. Collapse, revolution, new construction were not caused by this generation's literature; but they felt it, knew it, demanded that it happen. The chaotic elements of the time, the shattering of the old societal forms, doubt and longing, the voracious, fanatic search for new ways of living lives, all manifest themselves in the literature of this generation, with the same roar and the same savagery as in reality … but mind you, not as a result of the World War. It started before the war began, and became more vehement as it progressed."[72]

Kurtz also sees Expressionism not so much as a reaction to the war as the other way around, as perhaps the "most monstrous manifestation" of a spirit that desired to shape world history (12). He lists characteristic traits of the disposition of the time that were incorporated into Expressionism:

animosity toward Impressionism and Psychology; rejection of time constraints and the commonplace; orientation toward a primal, internal, spiritually and intensively-experienced reality; and the manifestation of a metaphysical determination to form and construct over time. He quotes oft-cited expressionist standard-bearer Kasimir Edschmid on the visionary artist of the day: "He doesn't see, he looks. He doesn't describe, he experiences. He doesn't reproduce, he creates. He doesn't take, he seeks. The chain of facts no longer exists: factories, houses, sickness, whores, screaming and hunger. Now we have visions of those things. Facts have a meaning only insofar as the hand of the artist reaches through them to grasp for [*in the original* 'comprehend'] what stands behind him [*in the original* 'them']. (16)"[73] Kurtz quotes imprecisely – perhaps a sign of the extent to which the traditional separation of background and foreground has become suspect. Surfaces don't conceal depth; they are themselves the expressive configuration of forces, distinguished by "the equilibrium of formal elements in space, the play of energies and intensities". (21) Using van Gogh as an example, this play appears as 'dynamic', 'buoyant', 'exploding', 'screaming', 'agitated', 'monstrous', 'alarming'. (20) It pulls readers, listeners or observers into the maelstrom of an experience. It suspends contradictions like those of art to reality, subject to object, temporality to eternity. It is reaction and action, apprehension of the present and utopia, in one.

What fascinates about Expressionism is its radicalism, its violence, its singular reality, its abstraction of concepts down to the most essential. "Abstraction" is one of the keywords in the contemporaneous art and culture discourse. Wilhelm Worringer, in his epoch-making 1908 dissertation, used it as the antithesis to "empathy", in describing a primal creative dimension that cannot be categorized as impression, or imitation.[74] He felt a driving force of early art was man's effort to liberate himself from the pressures of overwhelming reality – an effort which had largely gone lost in the modern era. In it, the natural and alive, the organic and psychological, dominated – following Theodor Lipps' formula that "aesthetic pleasure is objectified self-enjoyment". Artistic efforts from the Paleolithic to the Gothic and Baroque, on the other hand, were supposedly characterized by "style" and not "naturalism", whereby "style" for

Worringer refers to the dominance of abstract-geometrical creation, the prevalence of the two-dimensional over the spatial, concentration on the inorganic and crystalline, the individual, and the transcendent. Gothicism, to which Worringer dedicated himself in his postdoctoral dissertation of 1911,[75] is "the adolescence of European man" in the sense that it is the succinct embodiment of the struggle between two principles. It is at once a manifestation that "calls on our capacity for empathy", and also a de-naturalization of this manifestation, in the form of "expressive abstraction".[76] This idea easily provides a bridge to modern art, which Worringer early on tied to the idea of Expressionism,[77] claiming that renewed interest in the connection between expression and abstraction actualizes a "primal conflict" and signifies a (longed- for) turning point in history. Marked by the intellectual, the discordant, the convulsive and linear, it blends early and late periods.

Worringer's writings were initially recognized as scholarly works by artists rather than art historians. Wassily Kandinsky read *Abstraction and Empathy* as early as 1908, then tied together the category of abstraction with dimensions of inner reality, inner necessity and "inner sound" in his own, no less influential book *Über das Geistige in der Kunst* [*Concerning the Spiritual in Art*, 1912).[78] What was only implied by Worringer would become clearer after 1920: modern art's abstract tendencies hardly found their primary area of development in Expressionism.[79] Yet the question remains heated: is it best to react to the dialectic between contemporaneity and timelessness with the destruction or the concentration of form? *Expressionism and Film* too is infused with tension between presentness and primitiveness. This manifests itself not least in its passages relating current art to African and Paleolithic creations on one hand, and 'schizophrenic' ones on the other. Kurtz discusses the difference between cultural-archaic and intellectual-archaizing art (avoiding the folk psychology that played a prominent role with Worringer) in his characterizations of Nordic man, and cisalpine art. His primary concern is with formal similarities: "the handling of shapes, the reduction of elements to the static and highly-accentuated, the direction of the lines expressing movement, are all based on this distant Negro art ..." (26) An affinity lies dormant in these formal similarities: rejection of the coincidental, and a return to the meaningful, are the result of "an inner drive". (28) This figure of thought is key to Expressionism's self-empowerment: by maintaining that it is the necessary consequence of an historic situation, it promises to regain primal elements and free up the collective unconscious through its radical modernity. Its coalition with primitive, medieval and 'schizophrenic' art thus functions as both a symptom and a diagnosis – symptom of its 'Kunstwollen', which is concerned with the essential, and diagnosis of an era which is vacillating between old and new orders. In the words of Wilhelm Hausenstein: "All the arts which the expressionist spirit seeks out – and must seek out, due to a dialectical stroke of fate – share one decisive element, which we can characterize as the overpowering of the merely representational, the undetached present, the un-metaphysical, by the metaphysical".[80]

This metaphysical "compulsion" renders the coalition between epochs and cultures a source of fascination not only to artists and art critics, but also to psychologists and philosophers. Sigmund Freud establishes a connection between the spiritual lives of the Fauves and those of neurotics.[81] Karl Jaspers takes a stab at a pathographical analysis of Strindberg and van Gogh.[82] Fritz Morgenthaler hopes "to see, in the thinking of the Primitives, the origins of those things which have gradually crystallized into the objective features of spatiotemporality and concrete representation, to become formal or structural components of our consciousness".[83] In the works of someone like the mentally disturbed artist Adolf Wölfli, he discerns a quality which only begins to stand out in images by contemporary painters: the moderns "attempt to return to certain basic artistic elements by means of the systematic destruction of previous forms. But with Wölfli, such basic elements were revealed by an illness which destroyed his logic and other intellectual functions. They are doubtless rough and clumsy, and thus even more primordial. They reveal components of art's formidable cornerstones which certain modern directions still seek in their effort to get to the essence of things."[84]

While Morgenthaler tries to justify the ailing man's work as aesthetic and not (merely) pathological based on Ebbinghaus's objectivity functions, Kurtz casts doubt on this. He maintains that pictures by mentally ill artists are free from compulsory ties to form, and are therefore uncanny. Comparing an image by Chagall with the drawing of a schizophrenic photographer, he concludes: "The painting is the form-conscious creation of an artist; the drawing is the somnambulistic, assuredly reproduced humor of an anxious sufferer of desolate and harrowing dreams". (31) Worringer classified the scribbles of children as serving merely to satisfy psychological needs, but the abstract forms of early and African art as expressing a 'Kunstwollen' which require other means of description.[85] Similarly, Kurtz rejects 'sympathy' (19) when linked to "the usual psychologizing" as a method of apprehending abstract art. He contends this method fails to describe the specifically nonspatial spatiality that expressionist film is trying to achieve. As early as 1920, the architect and architectural theorist Heinrich de Fries saw film's potential for pronounced spatial depth – or lack thereof – as one of its characteristics. "The idiosyncrasy of film is that it must almost entirely do without the clarification of emotional states using conventional stage dialogue (and the more it does, the better it gets); these emotional states must be completely transposed to sensually comprehensible images. These images are no longer really images, since they comprise a storyline rather than Existence. They are images which have ceased to hold on to a moment in space for a period of time, but which show a series of moments in space for a short time. These pictures are no longer pictures, but space which comprises live events."[86]

Kurtz similarly emphasizes a vibrancy which is at once artificial and more than artificial. Yet as indicated, he writes at a time when expressionist shapes have been adopted by the home furnishings market, and things primitive and schizophrenic have become a familiar thrill. The new 1925 *Europa Almanac* (from which Kurtz took an illustration for his book) concluded with an illustration entitled "Europe as drawn by a madman".[87] At this point, understanding of the true nature of the world and its objects, of man and his soul (as augured by Expressionism), seems clouded. Kurtz concentrates on three dimensions of understanding: the creation, rather than the dissolution, of form; referentiality to the essential and life, rather than the everyday; and construction, rather than representation, of the world. And he expands his view to areas that are sidelined in other books on expressionist tendencies: architecture and music. Neither of these can be understood as paradigms of the mimesis which Expressionism rejects, thus providing little fodder for the expressionists' revolutionary gestures, animated as they are by opposition. Precisely therein lies their importance for Kurtz: they demonstrate the properties and limits of the expressionist phenomenon from the periphery. If architecture in the early 20s is considered the "manifest display of the intellect's mastery of material",[88] music is a paradigm for the "exploitation of the *inner* value of the phenomenon", a new realm in which "experiences are not acoustic, but *purely spiritual*".[89] Both imply subtle and direct relationships between lines, emotions and expressions: "A straight line leads the emotions differently than a slanted one; bewildering curves have different emotional correlations than harmoniously gliding lines; that which is rapid and choppy, and rises and falls abruptly, calls forth different emotional responses than the blended architecture of a modern city silhouette". (56)

But can this really be accomplished? In the case of architecture, the designs of the avant-gardists (Bruno Taut, Wenzel Hablik, Ludwig Mies van der Rohe, Hans Scharoun and others) who banded together to form the *Gläserne Kette* (*Crystal Chain*) from 1919 to 1921 stood out through their utopianism. Theirs were buildings for a time in which nothing could be built.[90] Kurtz too is more concerned with plans than their realization. In the design of a Salzburg Festival Theater by Hans Poelzig (who built the Jewish ghetto in Paul Wegener's 1920 film THE GOLEM), he recognizes passion and movement, though "his fantastic exuberance, his colorful rhythm, his marvelous execution of space and line ultimately [function] as a monumental work of applied art". (37)[91] On the other hand, he considers Mies van der Rohe's technically sober and aesthetically functional, yet radically innovative and intellectually significant design for an office building to be only loosely tied to Expressionism: "Nothing remains of Expressionism but a consistency of feeling about the world, which creates the work based on artistic preconditions, without regard to conventional solutions". (38) In the case of music (represented by the composer and music theorist Walter Harburger), the 'expressionist' is oriented to the movement away from the representational and toward the absolute: anti-impressionistic, anti-psycho-logical, anti-lyrical, anti-sentimental, anti-romantic. It leads to a concentration on "the line, the breath, the purely musical-geometric form". (40)[92]

Thus the expressionist swings between the absolute and the banal, between avant-garde hermeticism and mass medial effectiveness, between the superhuman and the universally human. Theatre, cabaret and dance, décor, furniture, and articles of daily use open up forms of articulation beyond literature and the fine arts, while simultaneously weakening Expressionism's radicalism and its vitality. "Intensely intellectual movements are only vibrant so long as they remain the strictly-guarded property of a combat-ready cohort. As soon as their tendencies stray into a broader circle, their tools lose their edge. Popularity always heralds the autumn of one's life." (50) Seen from the point of view of 1926, expressionist film finds itself in these autumn years. Its methods have become widely available and widely utilized, which has diminished their sharpness. This polarity is inherent to expressionist film and is not merely a result of its evolution. Indeed, its expressionist elements are threatening to come loose, either in the specifics of certain stylistic elements in commercial films, or in the absolute of the non-commercial avant-garde.

Thus the true period of the balancing act between mass medium and experimental aesthetic is short. Confined to the years between 1919 and 1924, it is symbolized by CALIGARI, which not only helped Expressionism cross over to the territory of film, but (together with theatre) made it socially acceptable. Following its premiere on February 26, 1920 in Berlin's Marmorhaus Theater, it was sold out for four weeks; two months later it was added to the programme again by popular demand; five years later it was reissued and became an export hit; the French saw it as the epitome of a new German cultural movement ('le Caligarisme') that promised to raise the German film industry to an international level and offer a counterbalance to American dominance.[93] It became the proto-type of the art film of the early 20s: "The history of the expressionist film in Germany is that of a series of repeats. Its beginning has never been surpassed. With improved technology, some forms have become more attractive and more effective, but this always involves a mere shading of the façade, while the blueprint remains unchanged. The attitude toward life has created a radical new form only with the "absolute" film. Expressionist film is a mere episode, perhaps valuable for having enriched us, but unproductive, since it failed to reach a level of universally provocative and transformative importance. *Caligari* struck a chord. Its successors have not managed to resonate more richly or more power-fully." (64) Indeed, most of the five other films that Kurtz singles out and that still form the core of expressionist film in film history had a difficult time in their day. Martin's FROM MORN TO MIDNIGHT (1920) apparently only screened publicly in Japan in 1922; his HOUSE ON THE MOON (1921) enraged the audience, leading the cinema owner to "post a sign to soothe and warn the theatre-goer as he entered";[94] Wiene's GENUINE (1920) was accused of being a display of applied arts rather than art; RASKOLNIKOV (1923) relied more on the rising star of Stanis-lavsky's Moscow Art Theatre than on the fading one of the expressionist art film. Leni's successful WAXWORKS (1924) confined its expressionist elements to one of its episodes.

All told, we have six films by only three directors, six films that are characterized by mixed styles. This makes it apparent why Kurtz carves out expressionist characteristics with one hand while emphasizing trans-expressionist tendencies with the other, relating art and commerce anew. Here is film's status as a mass medium which restricts the extent of its formal experimentation; there is its manifestation as an 'absolute art' which is not subject to such restrictions. His chapter on experimental films takes up about as much space in the book as the one on the actual expressionist films. Included are those in which expressionist elements are merely confined to individual sequences or effects: THE WILD CAT (Ernst Lubitsch, 1918), in which a grotesquely contorted set parodies "militarism, Balkan pomp and Eastern customs" (83); THE GOLEM: HOW HE CAME INTO THE WORLD (Paul Wegener, 1920) in which a Gothic dream set underscores the "flow of line, the power of physicality and the released energy of expression" (85sq.);[95] BACKSTAIRS (Leopold Jessner and Paul Leni, 1921) in which the light "[splits] the visual space

Hans Werckmeister, *ALGOL* (1920).

into abrupt, arbitrary spaces" (86); NOSFERATU (Friedrich Wilhelm Murnau, 1922), in which "overlapping visions of rats, plague ships, bloodsuckers, dark vaults, and black carts pulled by express-train horses work demonically together", counteracting "naturalistic reproduction" (84); and THE STREET (Karl Grune, 1923), in which the streetscape bears expressionist features: "The sets break apart irregularly; dark shadows bore holes in the houses; bright balls of light artificially inflate the atmosphere. Thus an unreal intensity, the *feeling* of night arises, the expression of which lies beyond naturalistic means." (86)

A number of other films which Kurtz and most of his successors overlooked could be included among these. The peasant chamber play TORGUS (VERLOGENE MORAL, Hanns Kobe, 1921) and the film based on Wedekind's EARTH SPIRIT (ERDGEIST, Leopold Jessner, 1922) were both scripted by 'expressionist' Carl Mayer, and they exhibit expressionist traits, at least in their light-shadow effects and interiors.[96] And there is also the futuristic dystopia ALGOL: TRAGEDY OF POWER, filmed shortly after CALIGARI by Hans Werckmeister, with the cooperation of CALIGARI set designer Walter Reimann, and featuring Emil Jannings. The film, a parable of rise and fall, expresses contemporary concerns about technology and power in a "bold mix of painted interiors, exterior shots and documentary material". The correspondingly artificial set, skewed and foreshortened, yet visionary and transparent ("a shimmering construction like a crystal formation [rears] up against the night sky") is tied to the utopian projects of the *Crystal Chain* avant-gardists.[97] Sometimes understood as a virtual allegory on the global power of the film, ALGOL played successfully in the summer of 1920 but was quickly forgotten.[98] When Lang's METROPOLIS premiered in 1927 (itself not without expressionist elements), hardly anyone seems to have recalled its forerunners – a sign that people wanted to put the expressionist paradigm behind them. Kurtz doesn't quite go so far as to distance himself from it. But he generates the potential effectiveness of his study by highlighting the outlook for Expressionism's relationship to film as well as its limitations. By not concentrating on the supposed core of Expressionism, he is able to put in perspective connections that will prove to be historically significant.

IV

In keeping with his methodical aspirations, Kurtz frames the chapters systematically, labeling them Architecture, Technology, Camera, and Lighting, then Directing, Script, Actors, and Set Designers. This is a circular and relaxed structure that leads from the material prerequisites to the stylistic overall phenomenon, allowing concreteness and abstraction to be placed in a dynamic relationship. Underlying this is his understanding of the artistic nature of film. Yet Kurtz does not seek to separate film from literature, theatre or photography, as did his predecessors. He means to profile its singularity, in view of its inherent documentary and mimetic potential. Reproduction on film, though it would seem superior to all other forms of medial representation by virtue of its 'authenticity', does not transpire at all naturally, but rather extremely artificially. The film images are selected, combined, and arranged by the director: "He reduces, simplifies, organizes with an eye to 'effect', arranges the dialogue, close-up, long shot, cut, extreme close-up in relation to each other – even though it might be intuitive – so that a thoroughly stylish whole emerges". (51) Montage is still considered a stylistic phenomenon and an 'interruption', in keeping with the state of reflection on German cinema. Even Balázs links his thoughts about 'image direction' to 'intermediate images' and will only build on ideas from French and Soviet discussions on montage starting in 1930, in *The Spirit of Film*.[99] The decisive point is that the artificiality of the organization of film as such establishes Expressionism's fundamental closeness to it.

Herbert Ihering had already noted this closeness at the time of the CALIGARI premiere: "The Expressionism and the film challenged one another. The film ultimately required excessive, rhythmic gesticulations; the Expressionism required the representational and variational capabilities of the screen."[100] These capabilities are a-mimetic or even anti-mimetic in Kurtz's view, and thus essentially artistic: they provide paths to the entelechy of the medium. If film's 'naturalism' is in principle cramped, then Expressionism is not fundamentally foreign to it, but instead presents an outstanding opportunity to showcase the "cinematographic art form". (52) Starting in 1920, interest focused on this art form. Yvan Goll had his eye on this 'cinema painting', in which all the arts played a role, "not only literature [...] but also painting, music, sculpture, dance",[101] while Kurt Tucholsky rejoiced that CALIGARI "Finally! Finally! is set in a completely unrealistic dream world".[102] Expressionist film is a particularly all-inclusive art form, and Kurtz emphasizes that it is upheld by a number of entities: the screenwriter considers the script's (spatial) effect, piloting the "artistic determination to get [...] toward an absolute" (122); the architect and stage designer set up the "intellectual preconditions for the events that take place" (129), creating the atmosphere which distances the viewer "from the everyday" (56); the lighting technician underscores "the jaggedness and energy of the lines", thereby accentuating or attenuating shapes (62); the actor, his gestures echoing "the oblique dips, sudden stops, and rolling curves of [his] environment", (126) becomes a non-naturalistic medium, revealing the constructive aspects of the world concept; the cameraman, by rotating and blending images, by "speed[ing] up and slow[ing] down movements", achieves a "stylization of dynamic relationships" (59); and finally, the director controls "the system of emphases, omissions, shadings, colorations, tempo regulations, and intonations that make the difference in the spirit and texture of the film". (116)

They all work together in expressionist film to achieve the emphasis on form that Kurtz marks as its salient feature. As a result of this emphasis, the eye falls on phenomena that can even now be said to constitute expressionist film: verticals, diagonals, slopes and distortions, light and shadow, isolated objects, and stylized, artificial action. Other things go unmentioned, such as the distinctive characters marked by dark romanticism and dreamy unreality, demonic obsessions with power, and modern desolateness. Or typical narrative elements: framing and doublings, weirdness and inscrutability, subjectivity and auto-reflexivity. These all play a role for Kurtz only insofar as he sees in the films the possibility of visualizing some idiosyncrasies of the period, via the refined artistic and technological methods of the moving picture. The concentration on "depths of emotion, sensations of movement, feelings of power, forces of intensity" (54) make it possible, he contends, to pierce through to the dark side of existence, "to the soul's most elementary processes". (55)

"Material that is removed from reality requires an abstract means of expression." (54)

Just as Expressionism in general is associated with a "certain disposition of the era", (63) so too is expressionist film in particular. Wherein lies this disposition? Kurtz points to the social and political revolutions of the time around 1919 as forming a dreamlike background for CALIGARI, rather than an aesthetic one; in 1919, Russian Bolshevism was accompanied by expressionistically-tinged propagandistic official art, and there was revolutionary unrest in Berlin. "The film itself seemed like a fever dream, undergoing its premiere at a wild time. Dark streets, the echoing barks of republican troop commandoes, the shrill cries of street orators. Behind the scenes, a city district plunged into darkness, occupied by radical agitators; the rattle of rifles, the clanging chains of soldiers, shots from rooftops and hand grenades …" (64sq.) He alludes here to the spring of 1920, when the Kapp Putsch caused Germany to hold its breath, and for a short time civil-warlike conditions prevailed. While Expressionism experienced a final boom, it simultaneously ran up against the limitations of the aesthetic. Yet Kurtz is no sociologist. He does not intend to study the collective psychology of the German political soul, as Kracauer will later. Questions of power and authority, and the relationship of the individual to society and state, are only hinted at. The contrast between old-fashioned bourgeois German film and current revolutionary events is not discussed at length – though the film's early reception suggests that it was precisely its out-of-time quality, and the decontextualization of its plot, that enabled CALIGARI to consistently attract new viewers.

But for Kurtz, dimensions of form are the main focus. They can be understood as an interface between a new way of shaping reality and a new way of revealing reality's defining energy. This is an interface for which CALIGARI, the book's common thread, forms a paradigmatic relay, between outside and inside, the dynamic and the static, surface and depth. One of Kurtz's singular accomplishments is that he recognized the film's potential. He has a specific sense of how CALIGARI shatters the dichotomy of insanity and reality – namely through its architecture.[103]

Robert Wiene, *The Cabinet of Dr. Caligari* (1919/20).

Kurtz's description of the dazzling set (by Walter Reimann, Walter Röhrig, and Hermann Warm), of the grotesque artistic spaces which function simultaneously as externalized emotional spaces, is unsurpassed. "The set seems to be built upon a creative concept; light is painted on, and mysterious ornaments emphasize its character, like foreign bodies applied onto paintings. Streets buckle and seem to fall on top of one another; the dullness, the narrowness, and the decomposition of the little city are just right. Trees are fantastically striving scrubs, naked, ghostly, the visual space shredding them into pieces as though they were frozen. Little building fronts fill the space like foreign bodies, crooked stairways groan with use, unseen powers open the doors, which are essentially greedy, cavernous orifices. The primeval nature of all apparatuses and all contrivances is awakened, created in geometric shapes out of time. [...] The verticals stretch out diagonally, houses confine themselves at tilted angles, and surfaces become rhomboids. Simple kinetic tendencies of normal architecture, as expressed through verticals and horizontals, are transformed into a chaos of broken forms; motion has taken on a life of its own. These crooked roofs, these inclined surfaces, and these tilted walls staring into the air, all represent a release of energy. A movement begins, leaves its natural course, is caught up by another and directed elsewhere, curves again, and breaks. Meanwhile, as brightness and darkness are unleashed, the magical light performs, constructing, dividing, emphasizing, and destroying." (68, 130)

While Kurtz places the accent mainly on surfaces, lines and movement, others emphasize the dimensions of depth and the physicality of the designed space, which they claim imparts "the feeling of permanently changing relationships between man, space, and destiny". This according to de Fries, who concludes: "In the *Caligari* film, the idea of space as an active phenomenon is firmly stressed. This space is a three-dimensional body; it is itself an actor with great power of expression. Everything that is concrete and corporeal is carved out, in an almost hyper-cubist way. The extremely harsh shadows are painted onto the set and placed in strong contrast to the tiniest glimmer of brightness. They sharply demarcate various bodies in space, such as street, house, square, room, furniture, and stairs [...] The effect of depth is elicited with unusual intensity, and is tied to the film's action since it is the most important actor within the space."[104] While depth effects emphasize the claustrophobic nature of the rooms, the crystalline archetype, so important to the expressionists,[105] appears here in the mode of the unfathomable, the distorted, the demonic, the opaque. Formally, the CALIGARI set is indeed related to the 'crystalline spaces' of Lyonel Feininger – who was influenced by Expressionism as well as Futurism and Cubism – and in particular to his Zottelstedt woodcut, which he produced shortly before the film premiered.[106] As Ludwig Coellen emphasized at the time, these spaces result from the search for a purely idealistic form, which "springs from the union of the subjectively Creative and the objectively Natural" and "is beyond the polarity of subject and object, something that exists unto itself, a purely material thing, in which the subjective is subsumed by the strict necessity of the principle, and the objective is completely de-materialized by the manifestation of this principle".[107] Yet with film, it is precisely the principle that moves into the twilight. Though elements of order are evident, it can only be understood as a distorted order. Kurtz suggests too that mathematical formulas and chaotic discontinuations

Lyonel Feininger, *ZOTTELSTEDT* (1918); © 2007 ProLitteris, Zurich.

do not contrast with one another, but rather reveal essential features of expressionist film: artificiality, vitality, fantasy, ornamentation, foreignness, disfiguration, momentum.

In this way CALIGARI approaches those 'absolute films' in which the narrative and the representational recede behind lines and motion. In Kurtz's descriptions, content becomes form, and plot becomes a pattern of lines; figures appear as a manifestation of the space in which they operate. This assessment lies thoroughly within the trend of the time. Numerous critics had pronounced the film's plot conventional, confused or minor, though they saw a great asset in its shaping of cinematic space and the dramatic expressiveness of the actors. Generally, this perception applied to the film's paradigmatic rather than its syntagmatic dimensions, and to its formal effects rather than its textual aspects.[108] Kurtz places the psychiatrist Caligari in the tradition of the demonic figures of dark romanticism, along with the majority of film critics.[109] Yet he does not pick up on aspects of insanity and loss of self, of crime and eeriness, which are tied to such a connection. To him, the characters are only marionettes within the composition: "figures without psychology, actors without apparent motives, humans who are simply animated forces, the gears in their brains invisible" (68). In fact, the film evinces obvious gaps in the development of its figures and plot, and it could scarcely get by without psychology. The triangle of Francis, Alan and Jane is defined by the two young men's desire, which briefly extends to the somnambulist Cesare. Caligari is obsessed, in the inner story, with the idea of crimes committed under hypnosis; in the frame story, he is convinced he can cure the psychosis of his patient Francis. The question of the inner and framing stories occupied contemporaries primarily with regard to the status of expressionist imagery. Many accepted that the frame led the main part of the plot "to seem to have sprung from the brain of a madman";[110] others felt it put a constraint on the film's artistic adventurousness. Ihering wrote: "Thus the vision of healthy reality is countered with the vision of diseased unreality. Or: insanity as an excuse for an artistic idea."[111] Roland Schacht thought that "the epilogue with its double sphere of explanations naturally reverses the dramatic effect of the [...] episode. One explanation [the showman Caligari is the director of the lunatic asylum] panders eagerly to the viewer; the other [Caligari's deeds are only a figment of Francis's imagination] is disappointing and boring."[112]

Kurtz finds too that the framing device is an admission of expressionist film's limitations, a gesture commenting on the otherwise incomprehensible. At the same time he sees it as an opportunity for film to develop around determinedly active people: "Caligari represents a fate outside the day-to-day, a feverish experience. The author legitimizes his own position to the audience by presenting it as the hallucination of a lunatic. But Mayer, for whom the term Expressionism means more than mere decoration, quickly grows out of this compromise. The material loses its mechanical bizarreness, remaining in the realm of matter-of-fact experience. It is pure poetic energy that lifts it to a metaphysical plane. Now the bourgeois loses its usual contour: the figures become forms with a compositional purpose. The external process becomes concentrated, metamorphosing into dynamic tension; the plot's sparseness allows it to dissolve into ever finer rhythmic relationships." (122) Kurtz was unfamiliar with the script by Carl Mayer and Hans Janowitz. As we know from the copy belonging to lead actor Werner Krauss (discovered in 1976 and published in 1995), it was different from Mayer's other scripts in that it was not written in the expressionist style.[113] In the script, we find that the frame story was not added by the director, as has been accepted since Siegfried Kracauer's influential interpretation (itself informed by Janowitz), but rather was altered in a characteristic way. Whereas in the script, a pair of friends look back on their experience with the tragic history of Dr. Calligari(s), the film plays with the narrative levels and the entanglements of a crime story in which night and sleep, ghostly, somnambulatory, and diabolical aspects prevail.[114] Imaginary spaces draw the viewers into the maelstrom of cinematic eeriness. Repeated iris fades in and out give them the feeling that the story they are following is not continual or clear. The intertitle lettering, consisting of jaggedly expressive individual letters, signals that this world, sprung from the "brain of a madman", is not confined to the inner story, but leaves its mark on the entire film.[115] The expressive architecture, paradoxically, can only be understood from a normal perspective as the expression of a twisted imagination; yet it appears to be an expression of that imagination. The unmistakable visual parallels of the final scenes, where first Caligari, then Francis, is held straitjacketed in a cell, prompts the question of which narrative level is generating identities and differences. In the final scene, the wall, with its painted-on light and shadows, appears merely whitewashed, indicating how easily the film builds up, then removes, suggestibility.

Kurtz shows as little interest in the transitions and the story's framework as he does in the shape of the letters, which are part of a cinematic space designed to affect the viewer. In 1920, the German-American author Herman George Scheffauer had already observed an expansion of space within the apparently two-dimensional, "not only in flight from the spectator; that is, towards the background, but into and beyond the foreground, to overwhelm the spectator with it, to draw him into the trammels, the vortex of the action".[116] The spatial artificiality which is specific to film creates in CALIGARI a no man's land between illusion and insanity, emancipating itself from literary models and from visual and

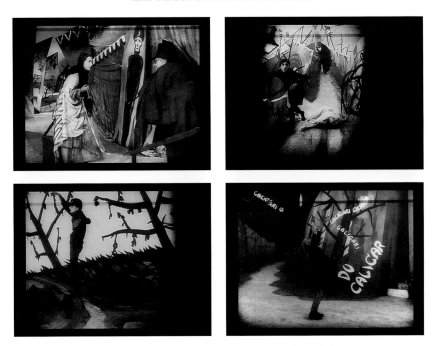

Robert Wiene, *THE CABINET OF DR. CALIGARI* (1919/20).

theatrical ones. At the same time, it produces a peculiar whirlpool effect: the perceived call to become one with the mystic translates to an identity crisis, which the film correlates to Francis's (possible) identity crisis, which renders the viewer's identity unsure. Through the perspective of a narrator who is recalling events yet is marked as not absolutely reliable, the viewer himself is driven to insanity – though it is a cinematic 'insanity', which renders an illusion the assumption that insane and genuine experiences can be kept separate.

Kurtz doesn't exhaust the film's wealth of themes – themes such as crime, power, doppelgängers, carnival, somnambulism, insanity, hypnosis, psychiatry, and mediality. Yet he sees CALIGARI as a model for what was to become "expressionist cinema", a cinema not imaginable without. As much as expressionist film design was a trend among outfitters at the time, its acceptance by film producers was encouraged by CALIGARI's success.[117] In 1920 alone, half a dozen films were produced that referred in some way to the expressionist paradigm. In addition to appealingly decorated films, there were a number of radicalizations. Karlheinz Martin attempted a film adaptation of Georg Kaiser's recent expressionist – and in itself cinematic – play, FROM MORN TO MIDNIGHT (written in 1912, first performed in 1917). According to Yvan Goll, who first saw CALIGARI in 1922, MIDNIGHT was adequate, "le premier film expressionniste cubiste".[118] It deals with the desperate yearning of an everyday character for a different, authentic life: a cashier is thrown off the course of his bureaucratic existence when he meets an elegant lady. He steals a great deal of money but doesn't manage to escape with her; rejected, he suffers through paradigmatic situations (racetrack, night club, a Salvation Army prayer meeting) that only increase his desperation. Betrayed to the police, he finally shoots himself. Martin executes this station drama, which centers on cycles of money and death, by accentuating the flatness, self-containment, and eventfulness of the cinematic image.[119] De Fries spoke of an "ecstatic agglomeration", in which "events from real life [...] become outrageously heightened and unreal".[120] Succinctly, he points out its difference to CALIGARI: "Abstract space, colourless and immaterial effects; no perspective-giving overview, but a two-dimensional background; no light and shadow effects, but black-and-white elaborateness; endorsement of the unsubstantial, symbolic, phantom-like. Space as a passive, restrained factor that does not live or itself take action."[121] Josef Aubinger, who saw the film in 1922 at one of the few special press screenings in Munich's Regina Cinema, wrote: "Its makers have succeeded in creating images that almost entirely supplant the word; and even when intertitles do appear, they make an impression on the brain through their singular slogan-like design, leaving the flow of pictures undisturbed".[122] The characters move before the painted sets, having cast off all naturalistic tendencies. They are, as Kurtz writes, "parts, elements of the decorative ideas, they too create the visual space; they are torn apart by the patches and bands of light that are painted on them". Yet to him, this also manifests the limitations of the experimental film: "This movement of humans who serve only as formal elements precludes the viewer's access to the film. What he sees are grimaces and contortions. He is filled with coldness, rigidity, and alienation." (46)

The expression of alienation is probably the film's intention, as one can now say from a greater distance. Martin, working with a small budget

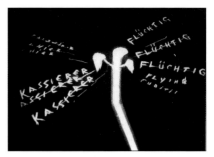

Karlheinz Martin, *From Morn to Midnight* (1920).

and a team used to working in a theatre environment, asks his lead actor Ernst Deutsch to perform jaggedly, discordantly, and according to his own rhythm. His face, mask-like, made up in extreme black and white, graphically displays the irreconcilable differences inherent to the world portrayed. This face simultaneously acts as a semantic counterpart to the "superimposed skull that the hallucinating cashier sees in the women's faces", and as a surface that reflects the "anticipation of insanity and death, in a (sexual) rush dearly paid for in cash".[123] On the other hand, the film's image composition and editing provide dissociation: the composition avoids the physical, malleable and harmonious, relying instead on primitive outlines, irregular structures, sharp contrasts, divided images and unstable structures – down to the lettering that renders the film itself a form of dynamic graphic representation, beyond CALI-GARI. In its use of bold dissolves and hard cuts, the editing confronts the viewer with the uncomfortable feeling that he is undergoing cinematographic existential analysis.

This was apparently more than the cinema owners of the time felt they could ask of their audience. Kurtz also viewed it as a failed experiment, unable to avoid the contradiction of expecting both artistic consistency and a captivating theatrical performance. The same was true for Martin's second attempt, THE HOUSE ON THE MOON (1921). Martin's script with Rudolf Leonhard conceives of a completely fantastical situation that illuminates the dark sides of earthly happenings in a different way. An astronomer lives in a mysterious house in which curious (creative) events transpire, and where strange figures reside on different floors. "The wife bears a daughter, Luna, who has a mysterious relationship to the moon, and sleepwalks. Conflict unfolds around her, causing the old man's ruin, death, insanity, and the destruction of the house." (76) Like other critics, Kurtz finds the film unsuccessful at settling the tension between construction and action. Though the film takes us away from 'daily reality', the "palpable psychological relationship between the figures" is abandoned. In order to make the unreal plausible, "the plot must flow from the characters and not bring in new moments of convolution from without". (75) For Goll, THE HOUSE ON THE MOON signals the end of expressionist film.[124]

So too with Wiene's GENUINE (1920), developed during the whirlwind of CALIGARI's success, and also based on a script by Carl Mayer. Kurtz misses in it a clear contour of characters and plot, a compelling urgency of events, and a set focused on the essential. Instead, the (also painted) décor has such an overblown decorative effect that it "injures the eye more than delighting it, with its inorganic chaos". (74) 'Inorganic' was one of the key words that Expressionism used to illustrate the dominant abstraction and artificiality that it strove toward. Now however, Kurtz also shows a preference for clarity and simplicity. In circulation as New Subjectivity since 1924, these assets are accompanied by intrinsic developments in film; a move toward stories set in the present day, a shift in ideas about plausibility and coherence, refinements in editing, nuance of action. From this point of view, GENUINE seems half-baked and gimmicky; fantastic, exotic, sensational and adventurous elements are more important than a coherent plot and characters. Even the script seeks to create imaginary spaces that are above ground and below, winding and crooked, and furnished with strange objects (such as a skeleton with a clock for a head); all this serves to highlight the effusive, histrionic acting.

The film's point of departure is, as with CALIGARI, a frame story: when a painter named Percy dreams that the female figure in a new portrait comes alive, her story unfolds. Abducted by an Oriental sect, Genuine is as attractive as she is bloodthirsty. She is bought and held captive by the eccentric Lord Milo in a strange house at the edge of a village, amongst tropical grottoes. Two young men succumb to her hypnotic

Robert Wiene, *GENUINE* (1920).

charms; first the barber's apprentice Florian, and then Milo's grandson Percy. Chaos develops around power, murder, love and jealousy, and finally enraged villagers storm the house. They kill the giant black servant and discover Genuine, fatally stabbed by Florian – the final consequence of a sexuality that is now held in check but still lethal.[125] Even early critics were divided on this film, pieced together as it was of fairy-tale fantasy and psychoanalytical archaism. They fluctuated between admiration for its fascinating world of images and rejection of its laboured mix of themes. In it, they saw the genre of great artistic and literary films firmly established, but also a dangerous movement toward elite films which were not geared toward the people.[126] One police censor rejected the film because "aside from a number of scenes which offend public morality, its contents and scenic design appear to be so senseless and so devoid of any logical or reasonable development, that it is anticipated to arouse vigorous displeasure in the public and could result in demonstrations".[127] Kurtz sums up: "GENUINE is an expressionist film because Expressionism was a success. But rather than a method of composition, it became the content of the film, so to speak. With this paradoxical discrepancy, the expressionist film faded. *Genuine* was the official proof that these films do not constitute a business. The 'boom' was over." (75)

At any rate, the paths that were opening up as a result of radical expressionist experiments with form were becoming clearer. One of these paths was the elaboration of psychological dimensions that made the expressionist plausible; another was the continued development of formal dimensions, which freed the abstract from its ties to logical action. Wiene (RASKOLNIKOV, 1923) and Leni (WAXWORKS, 1924) embarked on the first path. Wiene's Dostoyevsky adaptation, emphasizing "the problems of a state of twisted and tormented subjectivity", uses various means to provide an adequate translation of the material from book to screen: increased depth of focus strongly relates the character to the set; close-ups underline its Christian symbolism; trick montage conjures up visions that make evident "the student's feelings of guilt, fear and superiority". The film's use of thespians from the Stanislavsky troupe's ensemble allows it to develop a newly authentic acting style.[128] Whereas reviews consistently pronounced the film a masterpiece, Kurtz's judgement is more restrained. Occupied by its intensity of expression and the harmony of its architectural framework, he denounces its tendency to allegorize. Compared with Joe May's TRAGEDY OF LOVE from the same year, which is a straightforward, action-packed, suspenseful contemporary story, RASKOLNIKOV veers toward the forced 'Kunstwollen'. May "is not interested in expressing metaphysical fate; he is interested in the psychological distress of the martyred man, the informal cruelty of the investigating judge. What Wiene tries to force abruptly through decorative mood, through expressionist colouration, May attempts to allow the viewer to experience, in imperceptible psychological stages." (80)[129]

The expressionist element is pleasing when it is not an end in itself, but rather a functional component. So it is with Leni's WAXWORKS (1924, based on a script by Henrik Galeen), which in many ways can be seen as a true further development of CALIGARI.[130] Here too, the story begins at a carnival: a penniless poet is hired by a showman to write three stories about wax figures (Harun al-Rashid, Ivan the Terrible, and Jack the Ripper), which the film transposes visually. The film's origin lies even

Paul Leni, *WAXWORKS* (1924).

more firmly than CALIGARI in the literary imagination which, beginning with the gaze that focuses on and animates the wax figures, is transcended by the film itself. The film allows us to take part in a nocturnal orgy of writing, an imaginary dreamlike flow which leads to the blending of fiction and reality right when the plot approaches the present day (with Jack the Ripper). Blends, shifts, and distortions render outside and inside indistinguishable: "Natural shape is recklessly abandoned; the bound and released mass of spaces and lines, walls and bodies, crossbeams and projections, is represented most expressionistically. It is always full of energy that must explode, animated sets heaving themselves into space, voracious openings, and the dizzying ascent of stairs." (52) The plot's elevation to a 'metaphysical sphere' is acceptable because it remains integrated in the whole. When the poet finally escapes his dream pictures and wins the showman's daughter as his wife, the preceding spatial dynamization proves to be an expression of his psychological instability. Though this instability raises the question of the realistic nature of the images, it does not surrender to the intellectual balancing act between décor and plot. Expressionism has "subordinat[ed] its methods to its psychological purpose. It is becoming applied art. Leni has teased this capacity from Expressionism masterfully, thereby opening up a wealth of potential for its use in film." (82)

The same year in which Kurtz writes this, THE OVERCOAT is produced in Russia, directed by Grigori Kozintsev and Leonid Trauberg, and based on a script by Yury Tynyanov. The film's theatrical exaggeration, selective lighting and disproportional set led one reviewer to remark that it might be said to be "based on Caligari" rather than "based on Gogol".[131] In this film too there is an eclectic mix of stylistic elements; its inspiration stems not only from Wiene but from Wegener, Leni and Murnau (THE LAST LAUGH). Expressionist elements become routine in other films of the time, used to visualize emotional dynamics, illustrate subjective perceptions, or differentiate between various worlds. Henrik Galeen's 1926 remake of THE STUDENT OF PRAGUE, for example, transposed "Balduin's fears to a somber, 'expressionistic', sinister landscape" (designed by CALIGARI architect Hermann Warm),[132] following the connection between Expressionism and narrative cinema that, as Kurtz indicates, became dominant in the mid-twenties.

Similarities can be seen in two further examples from the period directly following *Expressionism and Film*. In SECRETS OF A SOUL (G. W. Pabst, premiere March 26, 1926), the first film to portray the successful use of psychoanalysis, expressionist elements play a role in dream sequences. During a thunderstorm, the chemist Martin Fellmann has a nightmare in which his cousin threatens him with a toy rifle while sitting in a tree. He flies through the air, experiencing strange things: trains run through one another, an Italian village pops up, a bell tower screws itself out of the earth, the bells turn into women's heads, the shadows of drummers create a dramatic atmosphere, and the bars of a prison cell rise into the sky, taking Fellmann with them. As mysterious as the individual sequences seem at first, their meaning becomes evident when they are explained by an analyst: they form a picture of a childhood disappointment that has led to impotence and childlessness in the man – not to mention murderousness and a phobia of knives, all finally overcome through analysis. Here there is no iridescent play between outside and inside, no oscillation between figure and ornament, but rather a rational order which must first be reconstructed. As a medium of reconstruction, the film offers itself, by isolating individually meaningful visual elements. Scenes from the lives of Fellmann and his wife, which are taken up again during psychoanalysis, appear before a white background, abstract and formalized; yet the abstraction and formalization aim not at the film's unique reality but its contribution to a "utopia of objectivity".[133]

A second example: METROPOLIS, by Fritz Lang (premiere: January 10, 1927). The aim here too was to "expose psychological processes" and to conquer "new cinematic territory", as Lang said during shooting. "The problems that are revealed here touch on questions from the realm of psycho-analysis. They require of anyone who tries to correctly interpret them a certain familiarity with psychology."[134] However, the finished film is far from a 'tale of the expression of the soul'. Though it sticks in a general way to the parable of the heart as the "mediator between the head and the hands", its vision of a society determined first by machines and powerful men, and finally by an early Christian humanitarian sensibility, has just as many thematic implications as it does contemporary prototypes. Many inspirations come from Murnau's NOSFERATU and FAUST. The film also shares with Georg Kaiser's trilogy KORALLE, GAS I, and GAS II themes like industry and automation, alienation and redemption. The images of the stream of humanity coursing forward, and geometric models of a collective free of domination, hearken back to socially critical expressionist artists of the second generation such as Karl Völker and Heinrich Hörle. The director's villa designed by expressionist architect Otto Bartning in Zeipa provides a direct mirror of the house of inventor Rotwang, appearing in the film as an odd relic within the skyscraper city.[135] Yet expressionistic elements are not restricted to a single case of borrowing. They also operate in the rigid motions of Freder (who seems to be sleepwalking at the time machine), in the fantastically huge dimensions of the amusement city, and in the lascivious dance of the false Maria. And they become part of the typical mélange of machine visions, city utopia, techno-eschatology, New Man ideology, formal aesthetics, and social and psychodrama, into which Expressionism was folded in the mid-20s.[136]

One review of the premiere pronounced it a "geometric film" on its way to being an "abstract film"[137] – an appropriate observation on METROPO-LIS' formal closeness to avant-garde tendencies, despite its contextual variety and narrative traditionalism. It is this, the second of the afore-mentioned paths, along which expressionist formulations permitted themselves to develop. A programme titled "The Absolute Film" played in matinees at the Ufa-Palast in Berlin on May 3 and 10, 1925, featuring films by Hirschfeld-Mack, Richter, Eggeling, Ruttmann, Léger and Picabia.[138] The organizer was the *Novembergruppe* [*November Group*], which had ties to the aforementioned *Crystal Chain* as well as the circle surrounding Hans Richter and Viking Eggeling, who had been collabo-rating on the magazine *G: Material zur elementaren Gestaltung* since 1923: Mies van der Rohe, Raul Hausmann, El Lissitzky, Theo van Doesburg, Hans Arp, Kurt Schwitters, Piet Mondrian, George Grosz, John Heartfield, Tristan Tzara, Man Ray, and also Walter Benjamin. The magazine intended to "create a forum for ideas that stood out following the Dada period, with Constructivism as a collection of all

Fritz Lang, *METROPOLIS* (1927).

cultural tendencies of the new era".[139] Film was also one of the ideators; the magazine's final, double edition from April 1926 was dedicated to it – and incidentally contains a review of the Kurtz book.

For avant-gardists of the time, the 'absolute', 'abstract' or 'illustrated' film demonstrated that the new medium had truly come into its own. In Richter's words, "To me, film means visual rhythm as portrayed using the tools of photo-technology; both are elements of a vision that creates by using the fundamental, regular components of our senses" (103).[140] The fact that these films could largely only be seen at two screenings in May 1925 provided Kurtz with a welcome opportunity to point out the limits of expressionist film, and he notes the limitations of a film art that cannot entirely do without the film industry's financial earnings. Whereas the commercial film favors objectivity, plot, and continuity in time, the avant-garde devotes itself to the play of shapes and the realization of 'pure' variations of Expressionism. On one side is the spectrum of non-representational films: the Eggelings who concentrate on abstract lines and geometric shapes, the Richters who play with surfaces, colour

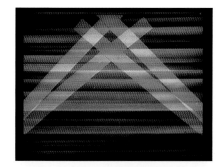

and motion, and the Ruttmanns who enchant us with dramatic se-quences, dynamic metamorphoses and organic suggestions. On the other side are the Dadaist-surreal films of Leger and Picabia, in which the representational and non-representational, the mathematical and the organic, the linear and the circular mix in new ways. What ties together the various approaches in Kurtz's eyes is that, with all their abstraction, they represent "the energies of modern, tangibly contemporary life"; (105) they are the graphic "expression of an artist carried along by the speed of modern movement, by the dynamism of cosmopolitan life", (109) and they saturate our sense of existence, within the parameters of its metaphysical constraints.

Admittedly the blossoming of abstract film was even shorter than that of Expressionism. The matinees garnered a great deal of interest, but also harsh criticism.[141] There quickly arose other independent efforts, includ-ing musically animated films (Oskar Fischinger), fairy-tale silhouette films (Lotte Reininger), satirical surrealist films (Germaine Dulac, LA COQUILLE ET LE CLERGYMAN, 1927; Luis Buñuel, UN CHIEN

Walter Ruttmann, *BERLIN: SYMPHONY OF A GREAT CITY* (1927).

ANDALOU, 1928), photographic art films that incorporated lighting design, and advertising films. Walter Ruttmann had experimented early on with light and shadow effects, designing the falcon dream in Lang's Nibelungen film, and demonstrating his ability to adapt to commercial requirements by making advertising films. As Kurtz correctly observed, he was the one most likely to build a "bridge to the world of daily experience" with his abstract films, by means of "feeling, decorative charm, and psychological effect".(107)

Kurtz felt his pronouncement justified when Ruttmann's BERLIN – SYMPHONY OF A GREAT CITY came out, on September 23, 1927. Based on an idea by Carl Mayer, it was filmed in collaboration with Karl Freund, who attempted for the first time to capture a day in the life of a metropolis. Accompanied by Edmund Meisel's specially-composed music, it begins with abstract wave motifs that transition into moving diagonals, which blend into railroad crossing gates, which a train passes by – a back reference to the aforegoing experimental opera. The film finds its own specific rhythm with regard to musical tempo on the one hand (andante, allegro, adagio, allegretto), and the fluctuating dynamics of daily existence on the other. This existence is marked by the usual and the unusual; work routines, means of transportation, crowds of people, machines, slaughterhouses, the zoo, a suicide; and finally the evening, with sports, free time, love, the movies, dance, opera, theatre and radio.[142]

In a review that appeared the day after the premiere, Kurtz was enthusiastic about this work that was perfectly shaped, thoughtfully composed, and "sustained by its strongly cinematic and rhythmic artistry; [...] the line reveals the hand of its composer-creator – there are chords, moderations, prestissimos, adagios, like in music. This is the metropolis as felt by an artist; it is a creation of iron, blood and light, pervaded by the powerful roar of life. It leaps from the film into the theatre and overwhelms it." He is fascinated by this form, which he suggests Ruttmann and Freund divine in the authentic, and which proves to be the intrinsic form of life itself. "The bonded energy in the front of a house, in the steep rise of a tower, is felt artistically, in a way that the free imagination of a painter is scarcely able to express; it is filmed from below and above, and in lateral shifts. We eavesdrop on people closely, in a way that no other film has managed. Startled, amused, perplexed, we observe the procedure of a man lighting a cigar. He acts naturally, with no idea he is being photographed by the small, scarcely visible Pathé camera. Nobody in it knew this film was being made; nobody paid attention to the grotesque, multifaceted drama of the process. And Freund is the classic maestro in his observation of the effects of light. Dawn over the city is photographed with tremendous artistry; the capture of light's emphatic, form-creating, punctuating and softening capacities is unprecedented. This film's photographic achievement will make German cinematography famous throughout the world."[143]

The film implemented ideas that were encapsulated in the buzzword of New Objectivity, the "cross-section" (*Querschnitt* was the title of a famous illustrated lifestyle magazine in the 20s that featured many New Objective photos). The film's images represent a time in which the everyday and the extraordinary adhere to the same rules, and real and medial experience interpenetrate. The film's cross-section is not so much an analytical as a suggestive one, made possible by the radical use of montage. It emphasizes formal connections rather than contextual associations: here pulsating crowds, there stamping machines; here workers on their way to the factory, there a herd of animals on their way to the slaughterhouse. And there are continuities of motion rather than differences in meaning: a roller coaster, a rotating spiral in a store window, a revolving door. In its quieter phases, its interest turns to people; old and young, rich and poor. But it is primarily directed toward processes and rhythms, as well as manifold forms of lettering and image. From the perspective of those on the political left, the film was superficial. It was even accused of betraying socialist ideals – symptomatic of a rift between Ruttmann and Mayer that had allegedly already started in 1927.[144] Siegfried Kracauer considers SYMPHONY to be "a summation of confused ideas, concocted by literary brains about a big city as they imagined it to be".[145] Taking stock of contemporary film, he notes: "Instead of penetrating its enormous object in a way that would betray a true understanding of its social, economic, and political structure, and instead of observing it with human concern or even tackling it from a particular vantage point in order to resolutely take it apart, Ruttmann leaves the thousands of details unconnected, one next to the other, inserting at most some arbitrarily conceived transitions that are meaningless. At best, the film is based on the idea that Berlin is the city of speed and of work – a formal idea that in no way leads to any content, and that perhaps for this reason intoxicates the German petit bourgeois when it appears in society and literature. There is nothing understood in this symphony, because it has not exposed a single meaningful relationship."[146]

V

What did these reservations about the formal mean for the perception of the Kurtz book? *Expressionism and Film* met with a favorable reception from contemporaries and early film historians. The back cover of *G: Zeitschrift für elementare Gestaltung* (*Materials for Elemental Form-Creation*), published by Hans Richter, boasted full-page ads by the book's publisher in its last two volumes of March and April 1926. The March edition also contains a short anonymous review pointing out that the book's "material is organized with scientific objectivity and artistic insight", and that it possesses "value far beyond the paradigm of Expressionism and film", "as an analysis of the universal artistic principles of our time".[147] The April edition even provides an excerpt from the book itself, an abstract of the "definition of the problem". Another review underlines the novelty of the approach, maintaining that art history has now caught up with film. It is "a backwards and forwards-looking art history", which "actualizes the forces of the Present in an idea". Kurtz "plays the melody of this idea in every key. Full beard and belly don't weigh down his opinions, which point to the presence of unified, driving forces in film as well as all areas of human expression. It is not at all film that is being diagnosed, but a world view."[148]

Others were enthusiastic, too. Vera Bern admitted to having spent "precious hours ... in the expressionist realm of Rudolf Kurtz".[149] A review in *Querschnitt* notes, "Kurtz says the best and most important things about cinema art that have ever been said, minus the idle café chatter, and he supports them with comprehensive pictorial material". The *Sozialistische Monatshefte* considered the book "perhaps the best that has been written about Expressionism. With a vigorous feeling for art and a similarly vigorous intellect, and above all from a thoroughly modern point of view, Kurtz manages to pursue all phases of Expressionism in the various arts."[150] The book quickly became a film history reference work. Rudolf Arnheim acknowledged his debt to Kurtz's groundwork, from the first line to the last, in his 1934 article "Expressionist Film".[151] Oskar Kalbus based the pertinent passage of his popular book on German silent film, published one year later, on the work of the expert. He considered him to have rendered the "architectural tendencies of the Caligari film completely understandable" – which didn't alter the distance he himself kept from expressionist film.[152]

Following World War II, Kracauer's position in *From Caligari to Hitler* (1947) gained prominence, in contrast to Lotte H. Eisner's in *The Haunted Screen* (1952). The books, both of which were written in exile and quickly became classics, concentrate on the German film of the twenties and early thirties. Both describe collective psychological dispositions; both mythologize or 'demonize' cinematic contents or forms. But they offer differing imaginary constructions of German film history. Whereas Eisner assumes a German condition of the soul that tends toward mysticism and magic, lapses into romantic, fantastic themes and motifs, and manufactures bizarre uncanniness by means of an elaborate light-and-dark style,[153] Kracauer attempts something else: to mark Weimar cinema as a subconscious 'prophecy' of the atrocities for which the German nation was responsible after 1933. He radicalizes the cinema as the scene of social and psychological (Oedipal) conflicts, drawing attention to the specific energy of film, which he channels one-sidedly, identifying fictional protagonists with topical constellations.[154] All the lunatics, machine men, tyrants and charlatans who flicker across Weimar screens seem to him to be prototypes of the dictators, charlatans and criminals on German soil who drove the world to war and destruction. "It is, at any rate, a strange coincidence that, hardly more than a decade later, Nazi Germany was to put into practice that very mixture of physical and mental tortures which the German screen then pictured."[155]

In such a context, there is no room for extensive reverence for Kurtz. Though Kracauer cites him about a dozen times – whenever he means to characterize Expressionism in general or an expressionist film in particular – his single explicit quote serves primarily to distance himself from his predecessor: "'Light has breathed soul into the expressionist films', Rudolf Kurtz states in his book on the expressionist cinema. Exactly the reverse holds true: in those films the soul was the virtual source of the light. The task of switching on this inner illumination was somewhat facilitated by powerful romantic traditions."[156] Their difference concerns the traditions and semantics of the formal dimension which expressionist film emphasizes. If Kurtz tries to bring to mind the films' aesthetic, stylistic and technical qualities, without delving into their meaning, it is precisely this political, psychological – even cultural-eschatological – meaning that Kracauer intends to make legible. Drawing on his experience with fascist mobilization and the orchestration of the masses, he hopes to discern the essence of a time in its forms and motions, now symptomatic of the crisis of that time. Where Kurtz sees the soul as the effect of the 'Kunstwollen' and a constellation of factors,[157] Kracauer thinks, inversely, that film is the result of a psychological disposition. Form criticism to him is just as blind toward the 'actual' impulsive moments of history as is the art film that emphasizes form. While CALIGARI remains fascinating in this respect, due to its thematic implications, the abstract film, especially in its German variant, now seems like an aesthetic escape into pleasantly visual music. "It was a music that, whatever else it tried to impart, marked an utter withdrawal from the outer world. This esoteric avant-garde movement soon spread over other countries. From about 1924, such advanced French artists as Fernand Léger and René Clair made films which, less abstract than the German ones, showed an affinity for the formal beauty of machine parts, and molded all kinds of objects and motions into surrealistic dreams."[158]

The trained art historian Lotte H. Eisner emphasizes precisely this dimension of form, tying it to the romantic tradition mentioned by Kracauer. She finds her central reference point in Kurtz's book; visibly fascinated, she cites it more than twenty times, using it to mine the myth of mystical-expressionist German genius. The 'soul' plays a key role here too: "In *Expressionism and Film*, Rudolf Kurtz points out that these curves and slanting lines have a meaning which is decidedly metaphysical. For the psychic reaction caused in the spectator by oblique lines is entirely different from that caused in him by straight lines. Similarly, unexpected curves and sudden ups and downs provoke emotions quite different from those induced by harmonious and gentle gradients."[159] Like Kracauer, Eisner attributes Kurtz's overly-elucidated formal concept of the soul to a metaphysical condition, which she sees as the essence of form criticism. Eisner takes the precise observer Kurtz as her model, furthering, amending, and 'inspiriting' his project. She chooses the chiaroscuro principle

LOTTE H. EISNER

l'Ecran Démoniaque

PANORAMA DU FILM ALLEMAND
ENCYCLOPEDIE DU CINEMA

Lotte H. Eisner, *L'ÉCRAN DÉMONIAQUE* (1952).

with which Kurtz closes his Caligari sketch as her springboard, but moves it from an aesthetic to an ideological category. For Kurtz, the crux lay in the expressionist stage and lighting techniques themselves: "The essential emotional content of these plummeting spaces and agitated lines flows from the light, which artistically separates bright and dark; when painted on, it animates the spaces and underscores their disposition". (68) Eisner transposes these contrasts to a model of a German world view, an ensemble of mythical visions: "the mist, the enigmatic chiaroscuro, the 'Kolossal', and infinite solitude" of the 'Faustian soul'. The cultural-historic thread of these ideas stretches from Novalis to Hölderlin and Jean Paul, to Nietzsche, Langbehn, and finally Spengler.[160] By reaching back to them, Eisner adapts a 'French' perspective on the 'German' film that Willy Haas had criticized in his 1924 *Caligarisme* article.[161] At the same time, she creates a metaphysical ancestral portrait gallery for Kurtz, her source of information: "Kurtz maintained that … Expressionism constructs its own universe, it does not adapt itself to a world already in existence. ('Every landscape', Novalis said, 'is the idealized Body of some form of Mind'.)"[162]

Yet Eisner does not merely cite Kurtz. She adopts his speech and his style, carrying her fascination with the subject over to her own language. This is especially apparent when she describes films that came out after Kurtz's book. Her observations on Fritz Lang's METROPOLIS (1926/27) read almost like a direct quote: "Lang handles lighting admirably … Light also plays a major role in the creation of the robot, as it had done in the symphony of the machines ... In this 'féerie de laboratoire' chemical retorts fill with a fluorescent light, coils of glass piping suddenly start to glow, zigzag flashes and sparks explode, rings of fire rise in the air. Lighting and superimpositions make the swirling mass of machines and ghostly elongated sky-scrapers sweep Fröhlich-Freder into a feverish nightmare, and he loses consciousness."[163]

Kurtz was not in complete agreement with Eisner's point of view. Just as he contradicted her about who was responsible for the Caligari film, which he saw firmly in the hands of Robert Wiene, he also took issue with her perception of his work: "You are missing the central premise of my book. For me, Expressionism is not an artistic genre, but the expression of a world crisis."[164] He must have found the factual perspective of the Polish film historian Jerzy Toeplitz more agreeable. Toeplitz mentions Kurtz approvingly several times in his *Geschichte des Films* (*History of Cinema Art*), emphasizing his insight on the epochal importance of CALIGARI.[165]

Reprinted in 1965, *Expressionism and Film* was recognized as forming the foundation of a "formalized method of analysis and evaluation" of films.[166] Though cited and exploited more than discussed and appreciated, and viewed as a historic expressionist document rather than a far-sighted analysis, it took on importance as an alternative to Kracauer's teleological view.[167] Some discovered that *Expressionism and Film* is "compelling reading", marked "by the author's congenial, affinitive empathy".[168] Some recognized the classic quality of the book. In 1981, an Italian translation appeared, accompanied by extensive materials (introduction, bibliography, filmography, film index, chronology, short biographies). In his introduction, Pier Giorgio Tone asserts that Kurtz clarifies a theoretically complex and confusing situation, extracting the reductionist schemes of an official culture dedicated to mass consumption. He claims Kurtz's discourse follows a two-pronged goal: to ennoble cinema culture and to identify "codes that make an autonomously motivated semiotic system out of film". He manages simultaneously to initiate a form of reflection that insists on the thematic and stylistic features of each individual film, and to set up the "premises for a theoretical foundation of film in general".[169] The French edition of the text, published in Grenoble in 1986, takes another direction. It honors Kurtz as a representative of the history of style (Worringer), as the generator of ideas for Eisner's *Haunted Screen*, and as the explorer of a genuinely aesthetic dimension of film, independent of the Kracauer school of socio-psychological analysis. "Kurtz reminds those who constantly seek parallels to Hitler in the shadowy manifestations of Mabuse, Nosferatu, the Golem and Caligari, that German cinema served a different purpose at the time, and raised different issues from the ones we raise today. [...] He merely aims to describe its aesthetic origins, and to analyze the magical use of light, dark, and white, which they took to new and powerful heights."[170]

Shortly before this we find traces of the impact of *Expressionism and Film* in the context of film theory. Gilles Deleuze cites it in the first volume of his work on cinema, *The Movement-Image* (1983), merely noting that, like him, Kurtz "developed the theme of a non-organic life in the cinema".[171] Yet starting with Deleuze's first sentences on German expressionist film, the Kurtz book seems to be his subtext. Though the difference between French and German film expression is reduced to a formula – here "more movement", there "more light"[172] – still there are flashes of what Kurtz had in mind when he emphasized "light" as the "emotional content" of CALIGARI, and marked the artistic differentiation between "bright and dark". (68) Deleuze's continued expositions on the constitutive opposition of light and dark move between Kurtz and Eisner: "light would be nothing, or at least nothing manifest, without the opaque to which it is opposed and which makes it visible"; it makes possible a "whole contrasting series of white and black lines" and even an entire "striped world".[173]

When Deleuze gets to the topic that inspires him most, the "non-organic life of things", he is completely under the spell of the German author. Individual passages function like abstract paraphrases, coming to a point at the exchange of the organic with the inorganic which Deleuze considers as crucial for expressionist cinema. Driven by an anarchic impetus, it celebrates the breakdown of the difference between authenticity and artificiality in favor of a new understanding of 'life': "*The non-organic life of things*, a frightful life, which is oblivious to the wisdom and limits of the organism, is the first principle of Expressionism, valid for the whole of Nature, that is, for the unconscious spirit, lost in darkness, light which has become opaque, *lumen opacatum*. From this point of view natural substances and artificial creations, candelabras and trees, turbine and sun are no longer any different."[174] Kurtz had similarly observed of CALI-GARI: "Two worlds meet that are constructed according to different ground rules"; "the organic touches on the geometrically-shaped"; the director attempts "to fit the organic material into the technically-constructed world". (43) The fantastical features of the set are the culmination of this principle. Kurtz: "Streets buckle and seem to fall on top of one another [...]. Little building fronts fill the space like foreign bodies, crooked stairways groan with use, unseen powers open the doors, which are essentially greedy, cavernous orifices." (44) Deleuze: "A wall which is alive is dreadful; but utensils, furniture, houses and their roofs also lean, crowd around, lie in wait, or pounce. Shadows of houses pursue the man running along the street."[175]

Both authors describe the aesthetic possibility of evoking a condition that precedes the contrast between authenticity and artificiality. The impression that the "primeval nature of all apparatuses and all contrivances" is awakened leads Kurtz to an archaic matrix in which the artificial and the natural, the inorganic and the organic are still undifferentiated. Deleuze writes: "In all these cases, it is not the mechanical which is opposed to the organic: it is the vital as potent pre-organic germinality, common to the animate and the inanimate, to a matter which raises itself to the point of life, and to a life which spreads itself through all matter".[176]

A very different structural approach to *Expressionism and Film* is taken up in more recent film history. On the one hand is the pragmatic question of the suitable systematization of expressionist film and more precise attention to various contexts: "It seems of utmost importance that we take up the differentiation between expressionist films and the productions containing individual expressionist elements – developed rather en passant by Kurtz – and that we demarcate and divide them into periods of German film production between 1919 and 1928. In this way we have the opportunity to put a stop to the inflation of expressionist attributions and also to appropriately designate mixed stylistic qualities."[177] On the other hand is the more general question of the connection between film history and the history of film theory. Thomas Elsaesser draws on Kurtz in his revision of Kracauer and Eisner, in order to (1) demonstrate, from the perspective of a competent contemporary, that the political environment surrounding the first expressionist films in no way compels pre-Fascist associations; (2) demonstrate that there was already an author in the 1920s whose sophisticated, style-based studies, inspired by Riegel, Worringer and Wölfflin, can be said to have influenced newer formal analyses – while avoiding future mythologization.[178]

Expressionism and Film looks attractive for several reasons. It avoids endlessly extending the term 'Expressionism' and declaring it a catch-all for German film production. It develops a variety of formal and thematic relationships. And it encourages investigation of the nuances in the conflict zone between authenticity and artificiality. Kurtz does not dissociate the works' authenticity from their techniques and structure; does not discern in them a tableau of meaning; does not anchor them in the political or socio-psychological disposition of a highly neurotic society looming 'under' or 'behind' the virtuosic artificiality of its productions. Nor does he suggest that expressionist stylization embodies a national authenticity which (clouded in secrecy) runs through the artworks of the age. If Kracauer and Eisner, each in their own way, generally regard the films as authentic precisely when they put artificiality behind them, Kurtz sees a tense 'ambiguity' between the authentic and the artificial that staves off claims to ideology. He thus awakens a sense of the semantic excesses and uncertainties that more recent film scholarly analyses have reinterpreted, with particular reference to CALIGARI. Written prior to the obsessive, grand narratives of the relationship between the psyche, film and politics, or the 'demonic' in the German soul, Kurtz's book offers us the opportunity to perceive the aesthetic complexity, formal refinement, and medial reflexivity of Weimar cinema, without losing sight of its social, political or economic dimensions. "In *Expressionismus und Film* (1926) Kurtz welcomed the convergence of a modern mass medium and a new art movement as an essential and integral part of the modernist imagination. For him, the expressionist film was simultaneously a product of aesthetic modernism and a response to the growing disenchantment with modernity. Like futurism, cubism, constructivism, and surrealism, Kurtz argues, Expressionism mediates between art and technology and seeks transcendence through an aesthetization of physical reality, [...] he relied on the most advanced technical means to enlist the new medium in a re-enchantment of the world."[179] Taken seriously as the eloquent and clear-sighted work of a connoisseur, *Expressionism and Film* has aged no more than its subject.

The translator wishes to thank Victoria Rummler (Paris) for translating the French quotations.

Notes

1. "Seul le filme pouvait réaliser cette nouvelle expression de la vie, faire vibrer ensemble en un rythme discontinu les hommes et les choses". Yvan Goll: "Films cubistes". In: *Cinéa*, No. 1 (May 6, 1921).

2. Lotte H. Eisner: *The Haunted Screen. Expressionism in the German Cinema and the Influence of Max Reinhardt.* London: Thames & Hudson 1969; *L'Écran démoniaque. Influence de Max Reinhardt et de l'expressionnisme.* Paris: Le Terrain Vague 1952; *Die dämonische Leinwand*, ed. Hilmar Hoffmann and Walter Schobert. Frankfurt/M.: Fischer 1980 (Fischer paperback 3660).

3. Lotte H. Eisner: "Stile und Gattungen des Films". In: Idem and Heinz Friedrich (eds.): *Fischer Lexikon Film Rundfunk Fernsehen.* Frankfurt/M.: Fischer 1958, pp. 263–265, here 264; cf. also Werner Sudendorf: "Expressionism and Film: the Testament of Dr. Caligari". In: Shulamith Behr, David Fenning, Douglas Jarman (eds.): *Expressionism Reassessed.* Manchester University Press 1993, pp. 91–99, here 91sq.

4. Sabine Hake: "Expressionism and Cinema: Reflections on a Phantasmagoria of Film History". In: Neil H. Donahue (ed.): *A Companion to the Literature of German Expressionism.* Woodbridge: Camden House 2005 (Studies in German literature, linguistics, and culture), pp. 321–341, here 324.

5. Cf. Michael Henry: *Le cinéma expressionniste allemand: un langage métaphorique.* Fribourg: Editions du Signe 1971; Trude Kronau: *Teatro e film nell'espressionismo tedesco.* Bologna: Leonardi 1971; John D. Barlow: *German Expressionist Film.* Boston: Twayne Publishers 1982; Francis Courtade: *Cinéma expressionniste.* Paris: Henri Veyrier 1984; Barry Salt: "From German stage to German Screen / Dai palcoscenici tedeschi agli schermi tedeschi". In: Paolo Cerchi Usai, Lorenzo Codelli (eds.): *Before Caligari: German Cinema 1895–1920 / Prima di Caligari: Cinema tedesco 1895–1920.* Pordenone: Edizioni Biblioteca dell'immagine 1990, pp. 402–423; Jürgen Kasten: *Der expressionistische Film. Abgefilmtes Theater oder avantgardistisches Erzählkino? Eine stil-, produktions- und rezeptionsgeschichtliche Untersuchung.* Münster: MakS 1990; Horst Fritz: "Ästhetik des Films im Kontext von Expressionismus und Neuer Sachlichkeit." In: Franz Robert Mennemeier, Erika Fischer-Lichte (eds.): *Drama und Theater der europäischen Avantgarde.* Tübingen, Basel: Francke 1994 (Mainzer Forschungen zu Drama und Theater 12), pp. 387–410; Thomas Elsaesser: *Das Weimarer Kino – aufgeklärt und doppelbödig.* Berlin: Vorwerk 8 1999; Thomas Elsaesser: *Weimar Cinema and After: Germany's Historical Imaginary.* London, New York: Routledge 2000; Paul Cooke: *German Expressionist Film.* Harpenden: Pocket Essentials 2002; Luiz Nazário: "Expressionismo Cinema". In: J(acó) Guinsburg (ed.): *O Expressionismo.* São Paulo: Editora Perspectiva 2002, pp. 505–541; Dietrich Scheunemann (ed.): *Expressionist Film: New Perspectives.* Rochester: Camden House 2003 (esp. pp. 1–31: Dietrich Scheumann: "Activating the Differences: Expressionist Film and Early Weimar Cinema"; pp. 33–71: Thomas Elsaesser: "Weimar Cinema, Mobile Selves, and Anxious Males: Kracauer and Eisner Revisited"); *Le cinéma expressionniste allemand. Splendeurs d'une collection* [Catalogue for the exhibit at the Cinémathèque française, Bibliothèque du film, 2006/07]. Paris: Édition de

la Martinière 2006; Ian Roberts: *German expressionist cinema. The world of light and shadow.* London: Wallflower 2008; Joachim Pfeiffer: "Dämonen und Vampire. Der frühe expressionistische Stummfilm in der Medienkonkurrenz". In: Georg Mein and Heinz Sieburg (eds.): *Medien des Wissens. Interdisziplinäre Aspekte von Medialität.* Bielefeld: Transcript 2011 (Literalität und Liminalität 4), pp. 223–241.

6. Bibliographical compilation: Paul Raabe (ed.): *Index Expressionismus.* Bibliographie der Beiträge in den Zeitschriften und Jahrbüchern des literarischen Expressionismus. 1910–1925. Vol. 2 Series A, Part 2. Nendeln/Liechtenstein: Kraus-Thomson 1972, pp. 1324–1328. Kurtz's shorter film journalism pieces are collected in: *Rudolf Kurtz. Essayist und Kritiker.* Mit Aufsätzen und Kritiken von Rudolf Kurtz und einem Essay von Michael Wedel. Munich: edition text + kritik 2007 (Film & Schrift 6).

7. Peter Panter (Kurt Tucholsky). In: *Die Weltbühne*, No. 3 (Jan. 19, 1912), p. 79: "Rudolf Kurtz, who left us poor men of letters for the money-makers, happens to be one of the finest writers; if only he'd tell us about all those who have passed through his long literary life, since he knows practically everybody who ever went to the old *Café des Westens*".

8. Paul Raabe (ed.): *Expressionismus. Aufzeichnungen und Erinnerungen der Zeitgenossen.* Olten, Freiburg/Br.: Walter 1965, pp. 121–124; here 123. The edition mentioned: F. T. Marinetti: *Futuristische Dichtungen. Autorisierte Übertragungen von Else Hadewiger. Mit einführenden Worten von Rudolf Kurtz und einem Titelporträt vom Futuristen Carrà.* Berlin-Wilmersdorf: A.R. Mayer [1912].

9. Else Lasker-Schüler: Letter to Franz Marc of Sept. 1913. In: Else Lasker-Schüler: *Werke und Briefe. Kritische Ausgabe*, ed. Norbert Oellers, Heinz Rölleke and Itta Shedletzky. Vol. 3.1: *Prosa.* Frankfurt/M.: Jüdischer Verlag im Suhrkamp Verlag 1998, pp. 303–306, here 305: "the venerable Berlin pashas: the GNU director Kurt Cajus Majus Hiller, Peter Baum, Ernst Blass, Albert Ehrenstein, Paul Zech, Hans Ehrenbaum-Degele, Rudolf Kurtz, blood caliph Richard Dehmel and Gottfried Benn"; letter to Herwarth Walden and Curt Neimann of June 29, 1912 ("Norwegian Letters"); ibid., pp. 200–204, here 201: "Rudolf Kurtz wrote me a letter today in the style of Kleist. But I detected a definite dissatisfaction in his lines, thus the circuitous route of the dispatch which I sent you, on the confederacy of Hiller, Hoddis, Kurtz, etc. etc. And he really did keep it curt, true to his intimate writing style".

10. Fritz Max Cahén: "Der Alfred Richard Meyer-Kreis". In: *Imprimatur.* N. S. 3 (1961/62), pp. 190–193; also in: Raabe, *Expressionismus* (note 8), pp. 111–116, here 112.

11. Ernst Blass: "Das alte Café des Westens". In: *Die literarische Welt*, Vol. 4, No. 25 (1928), p. 3sq.; also in: Raabe, *Expressionismus* (note 8), pp. 36–42, here 41 and 38 (see also a further report on the café by John Höxter, 1929, ibid., p. 314sq.).

12. Rudolf Kurtz: "Filmmänner". In: Max Mack (ed.): *Die zappelnde Leinwand*: Berlin: Eysler 1916, pp. 37–48 ; also in: *Rudolf Kurtz* (note 6), pp. 55–61: cf. Michael Wedel (ed.): *Max Mack. Showman im Glashaus.* Berlin: Freunde der Deutschen Kinemathek 1996.

13. He campaigned for the embattled author Karl May in an open letter in 1910, when the smear campaign against him was at its apex (*Der Sturm*, May 12, 1910). In an open letter to a Professor Kuckhoff, member of the Reichstag, he opposed attempts to limit the freedom of "sex education films" by means of moralistic censorship (*Lichtbildbühne* No. 23, June 8, 1918). In one discussion he is outraged that a work of art like Ruttmann's BERLIN – SYMPHONY OF A GREAT CITY should be "rubber-stamped by a German bureaucrat as commercially second-rate" and fail to be classified as a feature film (*Lichtbildbühne*, No. 229, September 24, 1927).

14. Peter Panter (note 7).

15. Quoted by Renke Siems: *Distinktion und Engagement. Kurt Tucholsky im Licht der "Feinen Unterschiede"*. Oldenburg: Library and Information System of the University 1995, p. 116; cf. also *Rudolf Kurtz* (note 6), pp. 96–99.

16. Cf. Paul Raabe: *Die Autoren und Bücher des literarischen Expressionismus. Ein bibliographisches Handbuch*. Stuttgart: Metzler 1992, No. 178, p. 293sq; *Rudolf Kurtz* (note 6), pp. 33–38, 250–254 (bibliography).

17. Rudolf Kurtz: "Die Geschichte des Filmmanuskripts". In: *Der Kinematograph*, No. 55 (March 20, 1934), No. 56 (March 21, 1934), No. 58 (March 23, 1934), No. 60 (March 27, 1934), No. 61 (March 28, 1934), No. 68 (April 10, 1934), No. 73 (April 17, 1934); also in: *Rudolf Kurtz* (note 6), pp. 126–141. Rudolf Kurtz: *Emil Jannings*. Berlin: Verlag der Lichtbild-Bühne 1942; also in: *Rudolf Kurtz* (note 6), pp. 141–172.

18. He held 24 percent of the shares; his fellow shareholder, the editor of the *Tägliche Rundschau*, Herbert Kilver, had 52 percent; see Stefan Marysiak: *Die Entwicklung der ostdeutschen Tagespresse nach 1945. Bruch oder Übergang?* Diss. Göttingen 2004, p. 294; cf. also Wolfgang Schivelbusch: *In a Cold Crater: Cultural and Intellectual Life in Berlin, 1945-1948*. Berkeley: University of California Press 1998, pp. 165–169.

19. Rudolf Kurtz: *Expressionismus und Film*. [Ed. H. P. Manz]. Zurich: Rohr 1965 [Film studies text 1]; Rudolf Kurtz: *L'espressionismo e il Film*. A cura di Pier Giorgio Tone. Milan: Longanesi & C. 1981 (Biblioteca cinema 18); Rudolf Kurtz: *Expressionnisme et cinéma*. Traduit de l'allemand par Pascale Godenir. Précédé de Rudolf Kurtz et l'esthétique du cinema expressionniste par Jean-Michel Palmier. Grenoble: Presses universitaires 1986 (Série: Débuts d'un siècle). For the importance of the book see Peter Wuss: *Kunstwert des Films und Massencharakter des Mediums. Konspekte zur Geschichte der Theorie des Spielfilms*. Berlin: Henschel 1990, pp. 149–161.

20. Hans Ulrich Gumbrecht: *In 1926: Living at the Edge of Time*. Cambridge/Mass.: Harvard University Press 1997.

21. Hans Sahl: *Memoiren eines Moralisten*. Darmstadt: Luchterhand 1984, p. 127; see also Ruth Glatzer: *Berlin zur Weimarer Zeit. Panorama einer Metropole 1919–1933*. Berlin: Siedler 2000, p. 296.

22. Ch. Gerlich: "Die Denkumschaltung durch den Rundfunk". In: *Funk*, 2 (1925), p. 209; also: Albert Kümmel and Petra Löffler (eds.): *Medientheorie 1888–1933. Texte und Kommentare*. Frankfurt/M.: Suhrkamp 2002 (stw 1604), pp. 210–212;

RUDOLF KURTZ

F.-H.: "Die Radio-Polizist-Maschine". In: *Technik für alle*, 15 (1925), pp. 110–112; also: Kümmel/Löffler, pp. 213–217.

23. Julius Bab: "Film und Kunst". In: *Zeitschrift für Ästhetik und allgemeine Kunstwissenschaft*, 19 (1925), pp. 181–193; also: Kümmel/Löffler, pp. 162–176, here 168.

24. Hans Bredow: "Eure Aufgaben im Rundfunk!" In: *Funkheinzelmann* (1926), also: Kümmel/Löffler, pp. 230–232, here 230.

25. Fritz Heider: "Ding und Medium". In: *Symposion: philosophische Zeitschrift für Forschung und Aussprache* Vol. 1, No. 2 (1926), pp. 109–157; reprint: F. H.: *Ding und Medium*, ed. and with a foreword by Dirk Baecker. Berlin: Kulturverlag Kadmos 2005.

26. Cf. Kümmel/Löffler's texts on A. K. Fiala and Rudolf Beranek.

27. Erich Palme: "Regie der Massen". In: *Kinematographische Monatshefte*, 6 (1925), pp. 1–7; also in: Kümmel/Löffler, pp. 218–224.

28. Siegfried Kracauer: "Calico-World. The Ufa City in Neubabelsberg". In: *The Mass Ornament. Weimar Essays*, ed. and transl. Thomas Y. Levin. Cambridge, London: Harvard University Press 1995, here p. 281sq.; "Kaliko-Welt. Die Ufa-Stadt zu Neubabelsberg" [1926]. In: *Das Ornament der Masse. Essays.* Frankfurt/M.: Suhrkamp, 1977, pp. 271–278, here 271; cf. Janet Ward: *Weimar Surfaces. Urban Visual Culture in 1920s Germany.* Berkeley, Los Angeles, London: University of California Press 2001, chapter 3.

29. Edmund Edel: "Wie Berlin zur Kinostadt wurde. Unvollkommene Erinnerungen". In: *Film Kurier*, No. 83 (April 9, 1926); cf. Dietmar Jazbinsek: *Kinometerdichter. Karrierepfade im Kaiserreich zwischen Stadtforschung und Stummfilm.* [Berlin] 2000 (http://bibliothek.wzb.eu/pdf/2000/ii00-505.pdf).

30. Béla Balázs: *Early Film Theory.* Visible Man *and* The Spirit of Film, ed. Erica Carter, transl. Rodney Livingstone. London: Berghahn 2010; *Der sichtbare Mensch oder die Kultur des Films* [1924]. Mit einem Nachwort von Helmut H. Diederichs und zeitgenössischen Rezensionen von Robert Musil, Andor Kraszna-Krausz, Siegfried Kracauer und Erich Kästner. Frankfurt/M.: Suhrkamp 2001.

31. Rudolf Harms: *Philosophie des Films. Seine ästhetischen und metaphysischen Grundlagen.* Leipzig: Meiner 1926, reprint Zurich: Rohr 1970 (Film Studies Texts 3), p. 186.

32. Anon.: "Expressionismus und Film von Rudolf Kurtz". In: *G. Zeitschrift für elementare Gestaltung* 5/6 (April 1926), reprint as: *G. Material zur elementaren Gestaltung*, ed. Hans Richter [Reprint ed. Marion von Hofacker]. Munich: Der Kern 1986, p. 98; English translation: *G: An Avant-Garde Journal of Art, Architecture, Design, and Film. 1923–1926*, ed. Detlef Mertins, Michael William Jennings, transl. Steven Lindberg, Margareta Ingrid Christian. Los Angeles: Getty Research Institute 2010; see also Karin Fest, Sabrina Rahman, and Marie-Noëlle Yazdanpanah (eds.): *Mies van der Rohe, Richter, Graeff & Co. Alltag und Design in der Avantgardezeitschrift G.* Vienna, Berlin 2014.

33. Cf. Heide Schlüpmann: *Unheimlichkeit des Blicks. Das Drama des frühen deutschen Kinos.* Basel-Frankfurt/M.: Stroemfeld 1990, p. 247; Friedrich Kittler: *Optische Medien. Berliner Vorlesung.* Berlin: Merve 1999, p. 246sq.

34. Georg Lukács: "Gedanken zu einer Ästhetik des Kinos". In: *Frankfurter Zeitung*

(Sept. 10, 1913); also in: Anton Kaes (ed.): *Kino-Debatte. Texte zum Verhältnis von Literatur und Film 1909–1929*. Munich, Tübingen: Niemeyer 1978 (Deutsche Texte 48), pp. 112–118, here 114sq. and 116.

35. Paul Ernst: "Möglichkeiten einer Kinokunst". In: *Der Tag*, No. 49 (Berlin, February 27, 1913); also in Kaes, pp. 118–123, here 119 and 122.

36. Kurt Pinthus (ed.): *Das Kinobuch. Kinodramen von Bermann, Hasenclever, Langer* [and others]. Leipzig: Kurt Wolff, 1914: New edition: *Das Kinobuch*. Ed. and with a foreword by Kurt Pinthus, with an afterword by Walter Schobert. Frankfurt/M.: Fischer 1983 (Fischer paperback 3688) pp. 22 and 27.

37. Bernhard Diebold: "Expressionismus und Kino". In: *Neue Zürcher Zeitung* (Sept. 14/15/16, 1916), citations from part 3 (Sept. 16, 1916).

38. Carl Hauptmann: "Film und Theater". In: *Die neue Schaubühne*, Vol. 1, No. 6 (June 1919), pp. 165–172, also in: Kaes (note 34), pp. 123–130, here 129.

39. Gertrud David: "Der expressionistische Film". In: *Der Kinematograph*, 659 (Aug. 13, 1919); see Kasten (note 5), p. 28.

40. Carlo Mierendorff: "Hätte ich das Kino". In: *Die weißen Blätter*, Vol. 7, No. 2 (Feb. 1920), pp. 86–92; also in: Thomas Anz and Michael Stark (eds.): *Expressionismus. Manifeste und Dokumente zur deutschen Literatur 1910–1920*. Stuttgart: Metzler 1982, pp. 487–493, here 489.

41. Cf. Hake (note 4), p. 331.

42. Dr. J. B. [J. Brandt]: "Expressionismus im Film. Die neue Kunst im Film". In: *Film-Kurier* (Berlin), Vol. 2, No. 4 (Jan. 1920), p. 1.

43. E. B.: "Das Cabinet des Dr. Caligari". In: *Der Kinematograph* (Düsseldorf), Vol. 14, No. 686 (March 3, 1920).

44. My (Dr. Wilhelm Meyer): "Filmkunst des Malers". In: *Vossische Zeitung* (Berlin), No. 110 (Feb. 29, 1920).

45. Anne Perlmann: "Das Kabinett des Dr. Caligari". Decla-Film. Press screening in the Schadow Theater. In: *Der Kinematograph* (Düsseldorf), Vol. 14, No. 696 (May 16, 1920).

46. Balthasar [Roland Schacht]: "Caligari". In: *Freie Deutsche Bühne* (Berlin), No. 29 (March 14, 1920), pp. 695–698.

47. Aros [Alfred Rosenthal]: "Der expressionistische Film". In: *Berliner Börsen-Courier*, Vol. 52, No. 79 (Feb. 17, 1920, early edition), p. 1.

48. Gerhard Schwarz: "Die Ausstattung im Film". In: *Germania* (February 22, 1925); cited in: Leonardo Quaresima: "Der Expressionismus als Filmgattung". In: Uli Jung and Walter Schatzberg (eds.): *Filmkultur zur Zeit der Weimarer Republik*. Munich and others: K.G. Saur 1992, pp. 174–194, here 178.

49. Robert Wiene: "Expressionismus im Film". In: *Berliner Börsen-Courier* (July 30, 1922); also in: *Das Cabinet des Dr. Caligari. Drehbuch von Carl Mayer und Hans Janowitz zu Robert Wienes Film von 1919/20*. Mit einem einführenden Essay von Siegbert S. Prawer und Materialien zum Film von Uli Jung und Walter Schatzberg. Munich: edition text + kritik 1995, pp. 149–152.

50. On the work of the painter: Piet Boyens, Gilles Marquenie: *Retrospectieve Frits*

Van den Berghe 1883–1939. Inleiding: Willy Van den Bussche. Oostende: PMMK 1999. On the uncanny in the early 20th century in general, see Nicolas Royle: *The Uncanny*. Manchester: Manchester University Press 2003; concerning film Burkhardt Lindner: "Stummfilmexpressionismus oder die Popularisierung des Unheimlichen durch das Kino." In: Jessica Nitsche and Nadine Werner (eds.): *Populärkultur, Massenmedien, Avantgarde 1919-1933*. Munich: Fink 2012, pp. 295–306.

51. Claus Groth [Julius Sternheim]: "Du mußt Caligari werden". In: *Illustrierter Film-Kurier* (Berlin), No. 6 (1920), pp. 2–5.

52. Balázs, *Visible Man* (note 30), p. 46; Harms (note 31), p. 156.

53. Cf. Quaresima (note 48), p. 176sq.

54. For example, a "naturalistic bed" is criticized for being found among expressionist "décor"; Herbert Ihering: "Ein expressionistischer Film". In: *Berliner Börsen-Courier*, No. 101 (Feb. 29, 1920; early edition), p. 8; also in: Ihering, *Von Reinhardt bis Brecht*. Vol. I, Berlin/GDR: Aufbau 1961, p. 374sq.

55. Ernst Angel: "Ein 'expressionistischer' Film". In: *Die neue Schaubühne*, No. 2, vol. 4 (April 1920), pp. 103–105; also in: Kaes (note 33), pp. 134–136, here 136.

56. Rudolf Arnheim: "Dr. Caligari redivivus" [1925]. In: *Film Essays and Criticism*, ed. Kristin Thompson, transl. Brenda Benthien. Madison: University of Wisconsin Press 1997, p. 111sq.; also *Kritiken und Aufsätze zum Film*, ed. Helmut H. Diederichs. Munich: Hanser 1977, p. 177sq.

57. Cf. Hake (footnote 4), p. 331.

58. Siegfried Kracauer: "Abhandlung über den Expressionismus". In: *Frühe Schriften aus dem Nachlass*, ed. Inge Belke. Vol. 9.2. Frankfurt/M.: Suhrkamp 2004, pp. 7–78, here 77.

59. Joan Weinstein: *The End of Expressionism. Art and the November Revolution in Germany, 1918–1919*. Chicago: Chicago University Press 1990.

60. Oskar Loerke: "Die sieben jüngsten Jahre der deutschen Lyrik" [1921]. In: *Literarische Aufsätze aus der "Neuen Rundschau" 1909–1941*, ed. Reinhard Tgahrt. Heidelberg and others: Schneider, 1967, pp. 333–337, here 336.

61. Robert Müller in: "Die Muskete". Special issue October 1923; cited in: Ernst Fischer and Wilhelm Haefs (eds.): *Hirnwelten funkeln. Literatur des Expressionismus in Wien*. Salzburg: Müller 1988, p. XIII (intro.).

62. Wilhelm Worringer: "Künstlerische Zeitfragen" [1921]. In: *Fragen und Gegenfragen. Schriften zum Kunstproblem*. Munich: Piper [1956], pp. 106–129, here 108.

63. Ibid, pp. 118–120, 122.

64. Cf. Franz Roh: *Nach-Expressionismus – "Magischer Realismus". Probleme der neuesten europäischen Malerei*. Lepizig: Klinkhardt & Biermann 1925. Roh doubts however "that the rather more abstract Expressionism and Constructivism have already been wiped out by newer alternatives" and adheres to the idea that "a change occurred around 1920" similar to the one of "around 1890". (p. 2sq.)

65. Balázs (note 30), English transl., p. 46.

66. The correspondence between Kurtz and Lubitsch is in the film museum in Potsdam (Collections/Estates).

67. The exchange of letters with Jannings is also in the Potsdam film museum. For the Jannings biography, see above, note 17.

68. Rudolf Kurtz: Paul Leni Obituary. In: *Lichtbild-Bühne* 226 (Sept. 21, 1929); also in: Hans-Michael Bock (ed.): *Paul Leni. Grafik, Theater, Film.* Frankfurt/M.: Deutsches Filmmuseum 1986, pp. 240–243, here 242.

69. Rudolf Kurtz: "Die junge Generation". In: *Die Aktion* 8 (1911), col. 241sq.; cited by: Franz Pfemfert (ed.): *Die Aktion. Wochenschrift für Literatur und Kunst.* 1911/1918. A selection by Thomas Rietzschel. Berlin and Weimar: Aufbau 1986, pp. 56–58, here 57. In the previous year he had formulated a piece of criticism on realistic aesthetics, in the first volume of Walden's *Sturm*: "Programmatisches". In: *Der Sturm* Vol. 1, No. 1 (March 3, 1910), p. 2sq.; also in Anz/Stark (note 40) pp. 515–518.

70. Cf. Friedrich Märker: *Lebensgefühl und Weltgefühl. Einführung in die Kunst der Gegenwart.* Munich: Delphin 1920; Eckart von Sydow: *Die deutsche expressionistische Kultur und Malerei.* Berlin: Furche 1920 (Furche-Kunstgaben 2).

71. Yvan Goll: "Der Expressionismus stirbt". In: *Zenit* 1, No. 8 (1921), p. 8sq.; cited by Otto F. Best (ed.): *Theorie des Expressionismus.* Stuttgart: Reclam 1976 (UB 9817), pp. 225–228, here 226.

72. Kurt Pinthus: Zuvor. In: *Menschheitsdämmerung. Symphonie jüngster Dichtung.* Berlin: Rowohlt 1920 [recte 1919]; new edition: Kurt Pinthus (ed.): *Menschheitsdämmerung. Ein Dokument des Expressionismus. Mit Biographien und Bibliographien.* Hamburg: Rowohlt 1959 (Rowohlts Klassiker der Literatur und der Wissenschaft. Deutsche Literatur 4), p. 28sq.; on the collection and context, David Roberts: "'Menschheitsdämmerung': Ideologie, Utopie, Eschatologie". In: Helmut Kreuzer (ed.): *Expressionismus und Kulturkrise.* Heidelberg: Winter 1983 (Reihe Siegen. Germanist. Abt. 42), pp. 85–104.

73. Kasimir Edschmid: *Über den Expressionismus in der Literatur und die neue Dichtung.* Berlin: Reiss 1919 (Tribüne der Kunst und Zeit 1), cited in: Best, *Theorie* (note 71), pp. 55–67, here 57.

74. Wilhelm Worringer: *Abstraktion und Einfühlung. Ein Beitrag zur Stilpsychologie.* Munich: Piper 1908, third edition (with an appendix "Von Transzendenz und Immanenz in der Kunst") 1910; used here in the new editions with new forewords, of 1948 and 1959. Munich: Piper 1976 (Serie Piper 122). On the context, Magdalena Bushart: *Der Geist der Gotik und die expressionistische Kunst. Kunstgeschichte und Kunsttheorie 1911–1925.* Munich: Schreiber 1990: Claudia Öhlschläger: *Abstraktionsdrang. Wilhelm Worringer und der Geist der Moderne.* Munich: Fink 2005.

75. Wilhelm Worringer: *Formprobleme der Gotik.* Munich: Piper 1911 (1920: 8.–12. editions).

76. Worringer: *Abstraktion und Einfühlung* (note 74), pp. 158, 160sq.

77. In his article "Zur Entwicklungsgeschichte der modernen Malerei" (In: *Der Sturm. Wochenschrift der Kultur und der Künste* 2, No. 75, August 1911, p. 597sq.)

he had used the term to defend the French Impressionists and the Fauves; also in Anz/Stark (note 40), pp. 19–23.

78. [Wassily] Kandinsky: *Über das Geistige in der Kunst.* Munich: Piper 1912 (quote here from the 10th edition, with an introduction by Max Bill, Bern: Benteli 1952); cf. Reinhard Zimmermann: *Die Kunsttheorie von Wassily Kandinsky.* 2 vols. Berlin: Reimer 2002, here vol. 1, p. 236sqq. On Worringer and Kandinsky as background for Kurtz, Joël Magny: "Expressionnisme et nouvelle objectivité: de Rudolphe Kurtz à Béla Balázs". In: *CinémAction*, 60 (July 1991), pp. 40–49. Worringer's idea of a "primal man's" two-dimensional creation of the world combined Hermann Bahr with Goethe's (and others') idea of a marriage between internal and external vision; H. B.: *Expressionismus.* Munich: Delphin 1919, p. 57sq., 68, 75sqq.

79. Cf. *Wege zur Abstraktion. 80 Meisterwerke aus der Sammlung Thyssen-Bornemisza.* Stuttgart: Edition Cantz 1988.

80. Wilhelm Hausenstein: *Über Expressionismus in der Malerei.* Berlin: Reiss 1919 (Tribüne der Kunst und Zeit 2), p. 31.

81. Sigmund Freud: "Totem und Tabu. Einige Übereinstimmungen im Seelenleben der Wilden und der Neurotiker". Leipzig, Vienna: Heller 1913 (initially a series of four articles in *Imago* 1912/13).

82. Karl Jaspers: *Strindberg und van Gogh. Versuch einer vergleichenden pathographischen Analyse unter vergleichender Heranziehung von Swedenborg und Hölderlin.* Bern, Leipzig: Bircher 1922 (Philosophische Forschungen 3); new edition Berlin: Merve 1998.

83. Fritz Morgenthaler: *Ein Geisteskranker als Künstler.* Bern, Leipzig: Bircher 1921; new edition Vienna, Berlin: Medusa 1985, p. 89 (citation by psychologist colleague Lewin).

84. Ibid., p. 90; cf. Edith Ihekweazu: *Verzerrte Utopie: Bedeutung und Funktion des Wahnsinns in expressionistischer Prosa.* Frankfurt/M., Bern: Lang 1982 (Beiträge zur Literatur und Literaturwissenschaft des 20. Jahrhunderts 4); John M. MacGregor: *The Discovery of the Art of the Insane.* Princeton: Princeton University Press 1989; Herwig Guratzsch (ed.): *Expressionismus und Wahnsinn.* Munich and others: Prestel 2003.

85. Worringer, *Abstraktion und Einfühlung* (note 74), p. 90sq.

86. H[einrich] de Fries: "Raumgestaltung im Film". In: *Wasmuths Monatshefte für Baukunst* 5 (1920/21), pp. 63–82, here 63.

87. *Europa Almanach. Malerei. Literatur. Musik. Architektur. Plastik. Bühne. Film. Mode,* ed. Carl Einstein, Paul Westheim. Potsdam: Kiepenheuer, 1925. Photomechanical reprint with an afterword by Wolfgang U. Schütte. Leipzig: Kiepenheuer 1993, p. 274.

88. Josef Ponten: *Architektur, die nicht gebaut wurde.* Vol. 1. Stuttgart, Berlin, Leipzig: Deutsche Verlagsanstalt, 1925, p. 11.

89. Kandinsky, *Über das Geistige* (note 78), p. 48sq.

90. Wolfgang Pehnt: *Architekturzeichnungen des Expressionismus.* Ostfildern-Ruit: Hatje-Cantz 1985, third edition 1998; Iain Boyd White, Romana Schneider

(eds.): *Die Briefe der Gläsernen Kette*. Berlin: Ernst & Sohn 1986; Idem (ed.): *Die Gläserne Kette*. Ostfildern-Ruit: Hatje-Cantz 1996; Rainer Hawlik, Sandra Manhartseder (eds.): *Farbenhäuser und Lichtgewächse*. *Wenzel Hablik, Paul Scheerbart, Bruno Taut*. Vienna, Bozen: Folio 2005.

91. Cf. Hans Poelzig. *Bauten für den Film*. Frankfurt/M.: Deutsches Filmmuseum 1997 (Kinematograph 12).

92. On expressionist music cf. Shulamith Behr, David Fanning, Douglas Jarman (eds.): *Expressionism Reassessed*. Manchester: Manchester University Press 1993, part III.

93. Cf. Émile Vuillermoz: "Réalisme et expressionnisme". In: *Les cahiers du mois*, 16/17 (1925), pp. 72–80, here 79sq.: "La décoration synthétique ou expressionniste doit etre pour nous une alliée précieuse. Si l'armée de la cinématographie avait une avant-garde […] on aurait depuis longtemps résolu ce problème. Tout notre effort devrait en effet tender à faire entrer dans l'Art Silencieux, les éléments techniques qui ont assuré le succès de la pensée et de la culture européennes dans les autres arts. Favoriser l'évolution du décor dans le sens que nous venons d'indiquer nous permettrait de reconquérir sur tous les écrans du monde le prestige dont les puissants industriels de Los-Angeles nous ont très habilement dépouillés". ("We must consider man-made or Expressionist décor as a precious ally. If there were an avant-garde contingent in the current film brigade […] the issue would have been resolved long ago. Our efforts should focus on infusing the Silent Art with the technical features that helped establish European thought and culture in the other arts. If we consciously developed set design in this manner, we could restore our prestige, which the Los Angeles industry's powers that be have so deftly stripped away, to screens all over the world".) For the reception of German cinema in the French press of the period cf. Marc Lavastrou: *La réception du cinéma allemand par la presse cinématographique française entre 1921 et 1933*. Diss. Université Toulouse le Mirail – Toulouse II 2012 (https://tel.archives-ouvertes.fr/tel-00793003/ [Aug. 12, 2015]).

94. Discussion in: *Das Tagebuch* (1921); also in: Ilona Brennicke, Joe Hembus: *Klassiker des deutschen Stummfilms 1910–1930*. Munich: Goldmann 1984, p. 190.

95. Contemporaries saw in this a "coarsened Expressionism, oysters for the people": Eduard Korridi: "Golem – Wegener – Poelzig". In: *Neue Zürcher Zeitung*, Vol. 142, No. 151 (Jan. 30, 1921), also in: Fritz Güttinger: *Kein Tag ohne Kino. Schriftsteller über den Stummfilm*. Frankfurt: Deutsches Filmmuseum 1984, pp. 323–326, here 323.

96. Cf. Jürgen Kasten: *Carl Mayer: Filmpoet. Ein Drehbuchautor schreibt Filmgeschichte*. Berlin: Vistas 1994, pp. 101–106, 150–157.

97. Dietrich Neumann: "Algol. Eine deutsche Parabel". In: *Walter Reimann. Maler und Filmarchitekt*. Frankfurt/M.: Deutsches Filmmuseum 1997 (Kinematograph 11), pp. 72–85, here 82, 80.

98. Balthasar (= Roland Schacht): "Kinol". In: *Freie Deutsche Bühne*, Vol. 2, No. 4 (Sept. 19, 1920), pp. 87–90.

99. Béla Balázs: *Der Geist des Films*. Halle/S.: Knapp 1930; new edition: *Der Geist*

des Films. Mit einem Nachwort von Hanno Loewy und zeitgenössischen Rezensionen von Siegfried Kracauer und Rudolf Arnheim. Frankfurt/M.: Suhrkamp 2001 (stw 1537), pp. 42–69; cf. note 30. On contemporary theories on actors, camera and montage: Helmut H. Diederichs (ed.): *Geschichte der Filmtheorie. Kunsttheoretische Texte von Méliès bis Arnheim.* Frankfurt/M.: Suhrkamp 2004 (stw 1652); Wolfgang Beilenhoff (ed.): *Poetika Kino. Theorie und Praxis des Films im russischen Formalismus.* Frankfurt/M.: Suhrkamp 2005 (stw 1733); Sergei Eisenstein: *Jenseits der Einstellung. Schriften zur Filmtheorie,* ed. Felix Lenz and Helmut H. Diederichs. Frankfurt/M.: Suhrkamp 2006 (stw 1766).

100. Herbert Ihering: "Ein expressionistischer Film". In: *Berliner Börsen-Courier,* 101 (Feb. 29, 1920, early edition) p. 8; also in: *Das Cabinet des Dr. Caligari* (note 49), p. 144.

101. Yvan Goll: "Das Kinodram". In: *Die neue Schaubühne* 2, No. 6 (June 1920), pp. 141–143; also in Kaes (note 34), pp. 136–139.

102. Peter Panter (= Kurt Tucholsky): "Dr. Caligari". In: *Die Weltbühne* 11 (March 11, 1920), p. 347f; also in: *Das Cabinet des Dr. Caligari* (note 49), p. 146sq., here 146.

103. Cf. Kitty Vincke: "Anstelle einer Errettung äußerer Wirklichkeit. Entwürfe von Walter Reimann für DAS CABINET DES DR. CALIGARI". In: *Walter Reimann* (note 97), pp. 50–65.

104. De Fries (note 86), p. 63, 69.

105. See Regine Prange: *Das Kristalline als Kunstsymbol. Bruno Taut und Paul Klee. Zur Reflexion des Abstrakten in Kunst und Kunsttheorie der Moderne.* Hildesheim, Zurich, New York: Olms 1991 (Studien zur Kunstgeschichte 63); Ulrich Johannes Beil: *Die Wiederkehr des Absoluten. Studien zur Symbolik des Kristallinen und Metallischen in der deutschen Literatur der Jahrhundertwende.* Frankfurt/M. and others: Lang 1988 (Münchener Studien zur literarischen Kultur in Deutschland 6).

106. Lyonel Feininger: [Zottelstedt] "Rathaus" (wood cut, 1918; 11.4 x 14 cm). In: *Ja! Stimmen des Arbeitsrates für Kunst in Berlin* (1919); Lyonel Feininger: "Zottelstedt" (wood cut, 1919; 23 x 27.8 cm). In: *Die Schaffenden* Vol. 2, No. 1 (1919); also in: Beate Jahn and Friedemann Berger (eds.): *Die Schaffenden. Eine Auswahl der Jahrgänge I bis III und Katalog des Mappenwerks.* Leipzig and Weimar: Kiepenheuer 1984, pp. 89 and 179 (no. 43).

107. Ludwig Coellen: "Lyonel Feininger". In: *Das Kunstblatt* 3, no. 4 (1919), pp. 130–137; also in Jahn/Berger, pp. 87–92, here 90.

108. Numerous passages from the contemporary literature: Fritz Güttinger: *Der Stummfilm im Zitat der Zeit.* Frankfurt: Deutsches Filmmuseum 1984, pp. 113–118.

109. Cf. Miriam Schütz: "Phantastische Romantik im deutschen Stummfilm". In: Walter Stock (ed.): *"Wahlverwandtschaften". Kunst, Musik und Literatur im europäischen Film.* Frankfurt/M.: Bundesverband Jugend und Film 1992, pp. 7–50; Bettina Gruber: "Hoffmann, Chamisso, Caligari. *Der Student von Prag* und *Das Cabinett des Doktor Caligari*: zu den romantischen Prämissen zweier deutscher Stummfilme". In: *E.T.A. Hoffmann Jahrbuch* 13 (2005), pp. 117–132.

For important material and interpretations of the film cf. Mike Budd (ed.): *The Cabinet of Dr. Caligari: Texts, Contexts, Histories*. New Brunswick, NJ, London: Rutgers University Press 1990; Richard Murphy: *Theorizing the Avant-Garde. Modernism, Expressionism, and the Problem of Postmodernity*. Cambridge: Cambridge University Press 1999, pp. 202–250; David Robinson: *Das Cabinet des Dr. Caligari*. London: BFI 1997; Thomas Elsaesser: *Das Weimarer Kino – aufgeklärt und doppelbödig*. Berlin: Vorwerk 8 1999, pp. 57–96; Dietrich Scheunemann: "The Double, the Decor, and the Framing Device: Once More on Robert Wiene's *The Cabinet of Dr. Caligari*", in: *Expressionist Film* (note 5), pp. 125–156; Francesco Pitassio: "L'antiquario alla fiera. Robert Wiene, Il gabinetto del dottor Caligari (1919)". In: Matteo Galli (ed.): *Da Caligari a Good Bye, Lenin! Storia e cinema in Germania*. Florenz: Le Lettere 2004, pp. 15–36; Anton H. Kaes: Shell Shock Cinema. Weimar Culture and the Wounds of War. Princeton: Princeton University Press 2009, chapter 2.

110. E. B.: "Das Cabinet des Dr. Caligari". In: *Der Kinematograph* (Düsseldorf), Vol. 14, No. 686 (March 3, 1920); republished with numerous other reviews of the Caligari film at filmhistoriker.de.

111. Ihering (note 100), p. 144sq.

112. Balthasar (= Roland Schacht): "Caligari". In: *Freie Deutsche Bühne* (Berlin), 29 (March 14, 1920), pp. 695–698; republished at filmhistoriker.de

113. Cf. Mario Verdone (ed.): *Carl Mayer e l'Espressionismo*, Rome: Bianco e Nero, 1969; Jürgen Kasten: Carl Mayer: *Filmpoet. Ein Drehbuchautor schreibt Filmgeschichte*. Berlin: Vistas 1994; Bernhard Frankfurter (ed.): Carl Mayer. *Im Spiegelbild des Dr. Caligari – Der Kampf zwischen Licht und Dunkel*. Wien: Promedia 1997; Michael Omasta, Brigitte Mayr, Christian Cargnelli (eds.): *Carl Mayer, Scenar[t]ist. Ein Script von ihm war schon ein Film*. Wien: Synema 2003.

114. Siegfried Kracauer: *From Caligari to Hitler. A Psychological History of the German Film*. Princeton: Princeton University Press 1947, pp. 61–76; new edition: *From Caligari to Hitler. A psychological history of the German film*. Edited and introduced by Leonardo Quaresima. Princeton, NJ: Princeton University Press 2004. *Von Caligari zu Hitler. Eine psychologische Geschichte des deutschen Films*. Frankfurt/M.: Suhrkamp 1979 (stw 479), pp. 67–83; new edition: *Von Caligari zu Hitler*. Neuausgabe. Übersetzt und bearbeitet von Sabine Biebl. Berlin: Suhrkamp 2012 (Kracauer, *Werke*, 2.1.). On the impact of Kracauer's interpretation, see among others Noel Carroll: "The Cabinet of Dr. Kracauer". In: *Interpreting the Moving Image*. Cambridge: Cambridge University Press 1998, pp. 17–25; Thomas Koebner: "Von Caligari führt kein Weg zu Hitler. Zweifel an Siegfried Kracauers ‚Master'-Analyse". In: *Diesseits der 'Dämonischen Leinwand'. Neue Perspektiven auf das späte Weimarer Kino*. Munich: edition text + kritik 2003, pp. 15–38; Thomas Elsaesser: "Weimar Cinema, Mobile Selves, and Anxious Males: Kracauer and Eisner Revisited". In: Scheunemann, *Expressionist Film* (note 5), pp. 33–71; Ian Roberts: "Caligari Revisited: Circles, Cycles and Counter-Revolution in Robert Wiene's 'Das Cabinet des Dr. Caligari'": In: *German Life and Letters* 57/2 (2004), pp. 175–187.

115. Cf. Christian Kiening: "Blick und Schrift. *Das Cabinet des Dr. Caligari* und die Medialität des frühen Spielfilms". In: *Poetica*, 37 (2005), S. 119–145; concerning

the film's mediality in general see Christian Kiening, Ulrich Johannes Beil: *Urszenen des Medialen. Von Moses zu Caligari.* Göttingen: Wallstein 2012, chapter 14; also Christoph Kleinschmidt: *Intermaterialität. Zum Verhältnis von Schrift, Bild, Film und Bühne im Expressionismus.* Bielefeld: Transcript 2012.

116. Hermann G. Scheffauer: "The Vivifying of Space". In: *Freeman* November 24–December 1 (1920); also in: Lewis Jacobs (ed.): *Introduction to the Art of the Movies.* New York: Noonday Press 1960, here p. 79; cf. Ward (note 35), p. 143.

117. On the reception history see Walter Kaul: *Caligari und Caligarismus.* Berlin: Deutsche Kinemathek 1970; Budd (note 109); Jürgen Kasten: "Besessene und Geschäftemacher. Zur Rezeptionsgeschichte von *Das Cabinet des Dr. Caligari*". In: Frankfurter (note 113), pp. 136–146; Jacques Aumont, Bernard Benoliel (eds.): *Le Cinéma expressionniste. De Caligari à Tim Burton.* Rennes: Presses Universitaires de Rennes 2008.

118. Ivan Goll: "Films cubistes". In: *Cinéa*, No. 1 (May 6, 1921)

119. Cf. Jürgen Kasten: "Filmstil als Markenartikel. Der expressionistische Film und das Stilexperiment *Von morgens bis mitternachts*". In: Harro Segeberg (ed.): *Die Perfektionierung des Scheins. Das Kino der Weimarer Republik im Kontext der Künste. Mediengeschichte des Films.* Vol. 3. Munich: Fink 2000, pp. 37–65; also "Film as Graphic Art: On Karl Heinz Martin's *From Morn to Midnight*". In: Scheunemann (note 5), pp. 157–172.

120. De Fries (note 86), p. 63.

121. Ibid., p. 78.

122. Josef Aubinger: "Münchner Erstaufführungen". In: *Der deutsche Film in Wort und Bild. Eine Kampfschrift für deutsche Kinokunst und -technik* 4 (1922); cited here by Inge Degenhardt: "Heimkehr in Zeitlupe". In: "Von Morgens bis Mitternachts". Munich: Filmmuseum 1993 (unpaginated brochure on the occasion of the screening of the restored version); see also Degenhardt: " 'Von morgens bis mitternachts rase ich im Kreise'. Vom expressionistischen Schau-Spiel zum filmischen Denk-Spiel". In: Ernest W. B. Hess-Lüttich and Roland Posner (eds.): *Code-Wechsel. Texte im Medienvergleich.* Opladen: Westdeutscher Verlag 1990, pp. 93–126.

123. Kasten, "Filmstil als Markenartikel" (note 119), p. 63.

124. Yvan Goll in: *Cinéa*, No. 88 (March 23, 1923)

125. Jung/Schatzberg (note 48), pp. 83–90, here 88.

126. A. F.: "Genuine". In: *Der Film* (Berlin), 5, No. 36 (Sept. 4, 1920), p. 28 (reprinted at: filmhistoriker.de): "They [the big art films] are simply creating a new genre. This cannot simply be dismissed as 'Expressionism', as was meant when 'The Cabinet of Dr. Caligari' appeared. We might rather classify it as a 'literary' film, if this term hadn't been so awfully worn out and misused. They are creating something on film like that which the works of Oscar Wilde, Stendhal and Hans Heinz Ewers have done for literature: these are creations of fine nervous tension whose hot breath nonetheless sweeps along both the literary connoisseur and the simple reader or viewer". Fritz Olimsky: "Genuine". In: *Berliner Börsen-Zeitung* (Sept. 5, 1920), also in: *Film und Presse* (Berlin) 1, Vol. 9 (Sept. 11, 1920), p. 222 (reprinted online): "Expressionism is now the great fashion, so it

was obvious that film would follow it as well [...] Decla deserves the fame of being the first to walk this path with CALIGARI, an experiment which without a doubt was very important and successful. Of course opinions on it were divided, but beyond that everyone admitted that this is new territory for film, that here there is a great, rich sphere of activity, a new way to develop our film art. Now the great question was, where would this development lead, should the film genre that started with CALIGARI be built up in a stark and extreme way, or would it be toned down after this rather strong prelude, and film art steered toward popular paths? Decla decided on the first route, and that is exactly wrong in my opinion. Film art must be and remain the people's art, our feature films must be tailored to the broad masses of people, first of all for business reasons, but if the people are alienated by the cinema because of an art film, then this film art is heading down the wrong path. This is such a film, it is completely out of the question that an average audience would understand such bluntly executed Expressionism, or even know how to come to terms with it. The simple man of the people is bound to be annoyed by his former favourite, the cinema, when he witnesses something like this".

127. Anonymous: "Ergebnisse der Polizeizensur". In: *Der Filmbote* (Oct. 16, 1920); also in: Omasta/Mayr/Cargnelli (note 113), p. 265.

128. Jung/Schatzberg (note 48), pp. 101–107, quote p. 106 and 105.

129. Cf. the generally popular film with its emphatic review by Peter Panter (= Kurt Tucholsky): "Tragödie der Liebe". In: *Die Weltbühne*, 43 (Oct. 25, 1923), p. 406.

130. *Das Wachsfigurenkabinett. Drehbuch von Henrik Galeen zu Paul Lenis Film von 1923*. Mit einem einführenden Essay von Thomas Koebner und Materialien zum Film von Hans-Michael Bock. Munich: edition text + kritik 1994 (FILMtext). On the film, Jürgen Kasten: "Episodic Patchwork: The Bric-a-Brac Principle in Paul Leni's *Waxworks*". In: Scheunemann, *Expressionist Film* (note 5), pp. 173–186.

131. Yuri Tsivian: "Caligari in Russland. Der deutsche Expressionismus und die sowjetische Filmkultur". In: *montage/av*, 2/2 (1993), pp. 35–46, here 43.

132. Brennicke/Hembus (note 94), p. 29 (quote by Klaus Eder).

133. Hermann Kappelhoff: *Der möblierte Mensch. G.W. Pabst und die Utopie der Sachlichkeit. Ein poetologischer Versuch zum Weimarer Autorenkino*. Berlin: Vorwerk 8 1995, pp. 51–74.

134. Ludwig Spitzer: "Fritz Lang über den Film der Zukunft". In: *Filmtechnik* Vol. 1, No. 2 (1925); quoted by: Fred Gehler, Ulrich Kasten: *Fritz Lang. Die Stimme von Metropolis*. Berlin: Henschel 1990, pp. 230–238, here 230/236.

135. Cf. Brennicke/Hembus (note 94), p. 134–142; Anton Kaes: "Metropolis: City, Cinema, Modernity". In: Benson (note 135), p. 146–165; Thomas Elsaesser: *Metropolis*. London: BFI 2000 (BFI Film Classics), pp. 17–22.

136. Cf. Timothy O. Benson et al.: *Expressionist Utopias. Paradise, Metropolis, Architectural Fantasy*. Los Angeles: County Museum of Art 1993; Francis Guerin: *In a Culture of Light. Cinema and Technology in 1920s Germany*. Minneapolis: University of Minnesota Press 2005.

137. Discussion in: *Film-Journal* (Jan. 14, 1927), p. 1.

138. Holger Wilmesmeier: *Deutsche Avantgarde und Film. Die Filmmatinee "Der absolute Film" (May 3 and 10, 1925)*. Münster, Hamburg 1994; *Der absolute Film. Dokumente der Medienavantgarde (1912 – 1936)*, ed. Christian Kiening and Heinrich Adolf: Zurich: Chronos 2012 (Medienwandel – Medienwechsel – Medienwissen 25).

139. Hans Richter: *Köpfe und Hinterköpfe*. Zurich: Arche 1967, p. 67; cf. *G. Material zur elementaren Gestaltung* (note 32).

140. Hans Richter: "Die schlecht trainierte Seele". In: *G. Zeitschrift für elementare Gestaltung*, No. 3 (June 1924), reprint (note 32) pp. 44–46, here 44.

141. For the history of the avant-garde film cf. Standish D. Lawder: *The Cubist Cinema*. New York: New York University Press 1975 (Anthology Film Archives Series 1); Malte Hagener: *Moving Forward, Looking Back. The European Avantgarde and the Invention of Film Culture 1919–1939*. Amsterdam: Amsterdam University Press 2007; Malcolm Turvey: *The Filming of Modern Life. European Avant-Garde Film of the 1920s*. Cambridge/Mass., London: The MIT Press 2011.

142. Overview of sequences, Helmut Korte: "Die Welt als Querschnitt: BERLIN – DIE SINFONIE DER GROSSTADT" (1927). In: Werner Faulstich, H. K. (eds.): *Fischer Filmgeschichte. Vol. 2: Der Film als gesellschaftliche Kraft, 1925–1944*. Frankfurt/M.: Fischer 1991 (Fischer paperback 4492), pp. 75–91.

143. Rudolf Kurtz: "Berlin. Die Sinfonie der Großstadt". In: *Lichtbild-Bühne*, No. 229 (Sept. 24, 1927); also in: *Rudolf Kurtz* (note 6), pp. 176–179.

144. A correction by Helmut Weihsmann: "Die Stadt im Hell-Dunkel. Konzept der Großstadt im deutschen Filmexpressionismus in Bedacht auf Carl Mayers Filmskripten". In: Frankfurter (note 113), pp. 64–86, here 75–79.

145. Siegfried Kracauer: "Wir schaffens". In: *Frankfurter Zeitung*, No. 856 (Nov. 17, 1927); also in: *Von Caligari zu Hitler* (note 114), Appendix 2 (German version only), p. 404sq.

146. Siegfried Kracauer: "Der heutige Film und sein Publikum". In: *Frankfurter Zeitung* (November 30 and December 1 1928); also (titled "Film 1928") in: *The Mass Ornament. Weimar Essays,* Cambridge/London, Harvard University Press 1995, ed. and transl. Thomas Y. Levin, here p. 318; *Das Ornament der Masse. Essays*. With an afterword by Karsten Witte. Frankfurt/M: Suhrkamp 1977 (st 371) pp. 295–310, here 308.

147. *G*, No. 4 (March 1926), repr. (note 32), p. 98.

148. *G*, No. 5/6 (April 1926), repr. (note 32), p. 130.

149. Vera Bern: "Expressionismus und Film!" In: *Schweizer Cinema* 16–17 (1929), pp. 3–5; quoted in Kasten, *Der expressionistische Film* (note 5), p. 16.

150. Both quotes from a collection of press reviews by the Lichtbildbühne publishing house, in an appendix to various publications, i. e. V. Pudovkin: *Filmregie und Filmmanuskript*. Berlin: Verlag der Lichtbildbühne 1928 (Bücher der Praxis 5), following p. 251.

151. Rudolf Arnheim: "Expressionistischer Film" [German-language typescript 1934

for *Enciclopedia del Cinema*]. In: Arnheim: *Die Seele in der Silberschicht. Medientheoretische Texte. Photographie – Film – Rundfunk*, ed. with an afterword by Helmut H. Diederichs. Frankfurt/M.: Suhrkamp 2002 (stw 1654), pp. 175–177.

152. Oskar Kalbus: *Vom Werden deutscher Filmkunst.* Part 1: "Der stumme Film". Altona-Bahrenfeld: Cigarren-Bilderdienst 1935, p. 107; also by Kalbus: "Expressionismus und Film". In: *Erwachen* (1928) [Special issue "Die Zukunft des Films"], p. 251sqq.

153. Eisner (note 2 [1980]), p. 17: "the inborn German liking for chiaroscuro and shadow".

154. Cf. Elsaesser, *Weimar Cinema and After* (note 5), p. 33sq.: "Kracauer […] tends to read the fictional protagonists of his films as emblematic representations of conflicts that have their reality elsewhere, or rather, conflicts that are fought by proxy in oedipal form because they cannot find their outlet in politics, organized labour or the street. At the same time, this makes Weimar cinema more radical than it would otherwise appear".

155. Kracauer, *From Caligari to Hitler* (note 114), p. 77.

156. Ibid, p. 75sq.

157. Kurtz, *Expressionism and Film*, p. 78: "No matter how man expresses himself on film, the moment he no longer expresses the soul of the viewer, contact breaks off, and understanding and interest cease".

158. Kracauer, *From Caligari to Hitler* (note 114), p. 68, footnote 10 (with reference to Kurtz).

159. Eisner (note 2), p. 21.

160. Ibid., p. 51f.

161. In discussing the phrasing of Pierre Gille, who in *Matin* of June 20, 1924 had referred to German film productions since CALIGARI as "psychopathic, unhealthy, demonically suggestive", Willy Haas noted: "But this is sheer nonsense. *Caligari* and *Destiny* are nothing more than the latest romantic offshoots, literarily speaking. […] One could […] just as easily and wrongly say that 'Caligarisme' characterizes the French mentality"; Willy Haas: "'Le Caligarisme'. Versuch einer Verständigung". In: *Film-Kurier* (June 28, 1924); cf. Quaresima (note 48), p. 188sq.

162. Eisner (note 2), p. 153.

163. Ibid., p. 233sq.

164. "Vous passez à côté de la thèse centrale de mon livre. Pour moi, l'expressionisme n'est pas un genre artistique, mais l'expression d'une crise mondiale". Letter to Lotte Eisner of March 23, 1958, quoted by Laurent Mannoni: "Lotte Eisner, historienne des démons allemands". In: *Le cinéma expressionniste allemand* (note 5), pp. 52–68, here 58. Eisner in turn admits in her memoirs that she quoted Kurtz frequently but found him difficult to read; Lotte H. Eisner: *Ich hatte einst ein schönes Vaterland. Memoiren.* Geschrieben von Martje Grohmann. Heidelberg: Das Wunderhorn 1984, p. 265sq.

165. Jerzy Toeplitz: *Geschichte des Films.* Vol. 1: 1895–1928. Berlin: Herschel 1972 (Polish 1955), p. 218.

166. *Filmwissenschaftliche Mitteilungen* 3–4 (1966), pp. 1082–1087; according to Kasten (note 5), p. 16.

167. Cf. Noël Carroll: "The Cabinet of Dr. Kracauer". In: *Millennium*, 2 (Spring/Summer 1978), pp. 77–85; Barry Salt: "From Caligari to Who?" In: *Sight and Sound*, Vol. 48, No. 2 (1979), pp. 119–123; Thomas Koebner: "Von Caligari führt kein Weg zu Hitler. Zweifel an Siegfried Kracauers 'Master'-Analyse". In: Koebner and others (eds.): *Diesseits der 'Dämonischen Leinwand.' Neue Perspektiven auf das späte Weimarer Kino*. Munich: Edition text + kritik im Richard Boorberg Verlag 2003, pp. 15–40.

168. Richard Brinkmann: *Expressionismus. Internationale Forschung zu einem internationalen Phänomen*. Stuttgart: Metzler 1980, p. 30.

169. Kurtz, *L'espressionisimo e il film* (note 19), p. XVII.

170. "A tous ceux qui ne peuvent voir surgir l'ombre de Mabuse, de Nosferatu, du Golem ou de Caligari sans s'interroger sur son rapport à Hitler, Kurtz rappelle que le cinéma allemand de cette époque avait d'autres exigences, se posait d'autres questions que celles que nous y cherchons aujourd'hui. [...] Il s'efforce seulement d'en décrire la genèse esthétique, d'analyser cette magie de la lumière, du noir et du blanc, qu'ils surent élever à une puissance inégalée". Kurtz, *Expressionnisme et cinéma* (note 25), introduction by Jean-Michel Palmier, p. 36. A good evaluation also in Magny (note 78).

171. Gilles Deleuze: *Cinema I, The Movement-Image*, transl. Hugh Tomlinson and Barbara Habberjam. London, New York: Bloomsbury Publishing 2013, p. 225; *Cinema I. L'image-mouvement*. Paris: Les editions de minuit 1983.

172. Ibid., English transl., p. 49.

173. Ibid., p. 49sq.

174. Ibid., p. 50sq.

175. Ibid., p. 51.

176. Ibid., p. 51.

177. Kasten, *Der expressionistische Film* (note 5), p. 11sq. (evaluating the book as a first attempt at "a comprehensive representation of expressionist film"); on Kurtz's accomplishment, see also Sudendorf (note 5), Scheunemann (note 5), Wust (note 19). Quaresima (note 48) admits that Kurtz's book contains a "correct assessment of indicators of expressionist style (pre-eminence of the director, stylistic unity, representation of a sphere of life that deviates from the everyday)", but categorizes it as a "very overrated and also rather confused work" due to its "narrow interpretation of expressionist film".

178. Elsaesser, *Weimar Cinema and After* (note 5), pp. 22, 26, 71–72, 96.

179. Hake (note 4), p. 329.

List of Illustrations

Afterword

Index